W9-BNR-046

Best Editorial Cartoons of the Year

W

HOUSE
SENATE

RUMSFELD

BEST EDITORIAL CARTOONS OF THE YEAR

2007 EDITION

Edited by
CHARLES BROOKS

PELICAN PUBLISHING COMPANY
GRETNA 2007

Library of Congress Serial Catalog Data

Best Editorial Cartoons, 1972-
Gretna [La.] Pelican Pub. Co.
v. 35 cm annual—
"A pictorial history of the year."

United States—Politics and government—
1969—Caricatures and cartoons—Periodicals.
E839.5B45 320.9'7309240207 73-643645
ISSN 0091-2220   MARC-S

Printed in the United States of America

Published by Pelican Publishing Company, Inc.
1000 Burmaster Street, Gretna, Louisiana 70053

Contents

Award-Winning Cartoons

2006 PULITZER PRIZE

MIKE LUCKOVICH

Editorial Cartoonist
Atlanta Journal-Constitution

Born in Seattle, Washington, 1960; graduated from the University of Washington in 1982 with a degree in political science; editorial cartoonist for the *Greenville News* in South Carolina and the New Orleans *Times-Picayune* before moving to the Atlanta *Journal-Constitution;* previous winner of the Pulitzer Prize in 1995, the Reuben Award, the Thomas Nast Award, the National Headliner Award, and the Sigma Delta Chi Award; shared the 2006 Overseas Press Club Award; nationally syndicated in some 150 newspapers.

MIKE LUCKOVICH

Editorial Cartoonist
Atlanta Journal-Constitution

2005 SIGMA DELTA CHI AWARD
(Awarded in 2006)

MIKE LUCKOVICH

Editorial Cartoonist
Atlanta Journal-Constitution

2006 OVERSEAS PRESS CLUB AWARD

MIKE LUCKOVICH

Editorial Cartoonist
Atlanta Journal-Constitution

CLAY BENNETT

Editorial Cartoonist
The Christian Science Monitor

Born in Clinton, South Carolina, 1958; graduated from the University of North Alabama in 1980; editorial cartoonist for the St. Petersburg *Times,* 1981-84, and *The Christian Science Monitor,* 1998-present; previous winner of the John Fischetti Award, the Sigma Delta Chi Award, the National Journalism Award, the National Headliner Award, and the Pulitzer Prize; shared the 2006 Overseas Press Club Award.

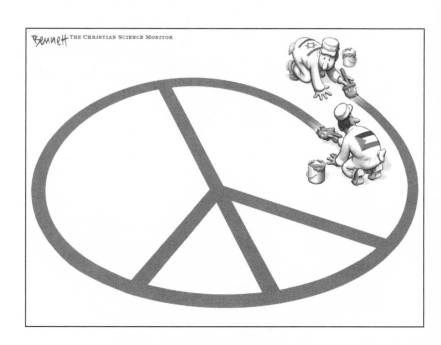

2006 BERRYMAN AWARD

JIMMY MARGULIES

Editorial Cartoonist
The Hackensack (N.J.) Record

Born in Brooklyn, New York, in 1951; graduate of Carnegie-Mellon University in 1973; editorial cartoonist for the Army Times / Journal Newspapers of Maryland and Virginia, 1980-81, the Journal Newspapers, 1981-84, the *Houston Post,* 1984-90, and *The Record,* 1990-present; previous winner of the National Headliner Award and the John Fischetti Award, both in 1996.

2006 NATIONAL JOURNALISM AWARD

MICHAEL RAMIREZ

Editorial Cartoonist and Senior Editor
Investor's Business Daily

Born in Tokyo in 1961; graduated from the University of California at
Irvine in 1984; editorial cartoonist for Baker Communications / *Palos
Verdes Penninsula News,* 1983-90, the San Clemente *Daily Sun* and *Post,*
1989-90, the Memphis *Commercial Appeal,* 1990-97, the *Los Angeles
Times,* 1997-2005, and *Investor's Business Daily,* 2005-present; winner
of the Pulitzer Prize, 1994, and the Sigma Delta Chi Award, 1995 and
1997; served as president of the Association of American Editorial Cartoonists, 1998.

Best Editorial Cartoons of the Year

SCOTT STANTIS
Courtesy Birmingham News

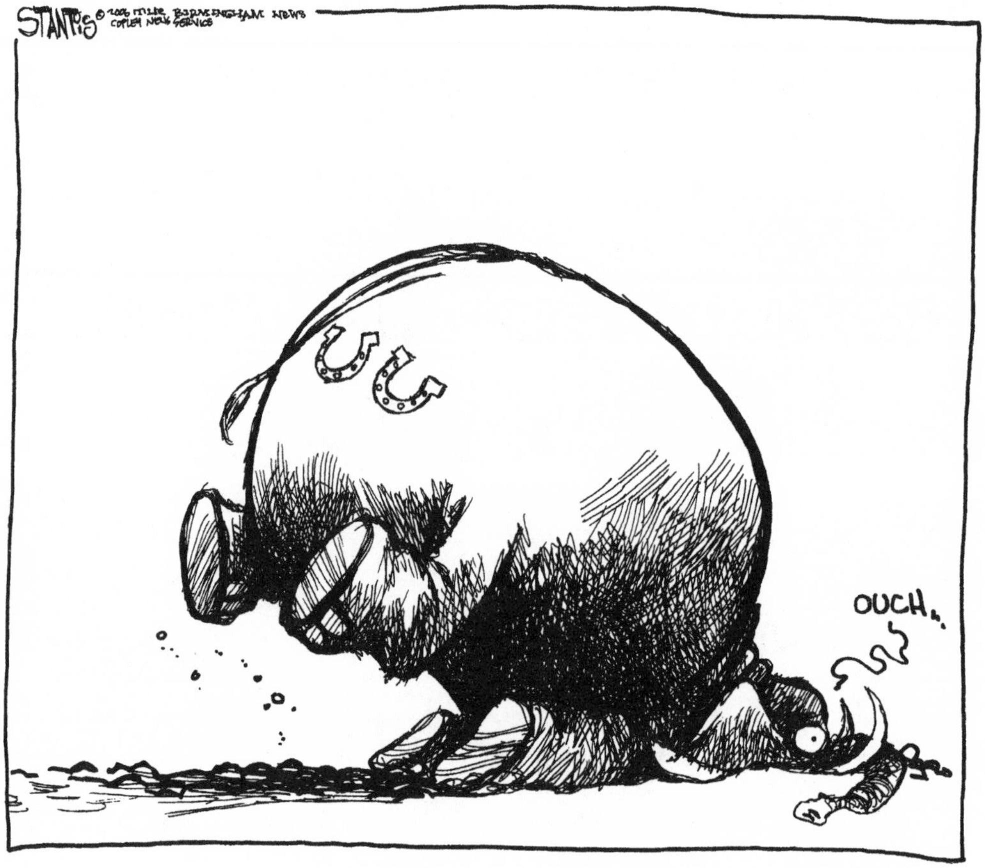
STANTIS
OUCH..

MIKE KEEFE
Courtesy Denver Post

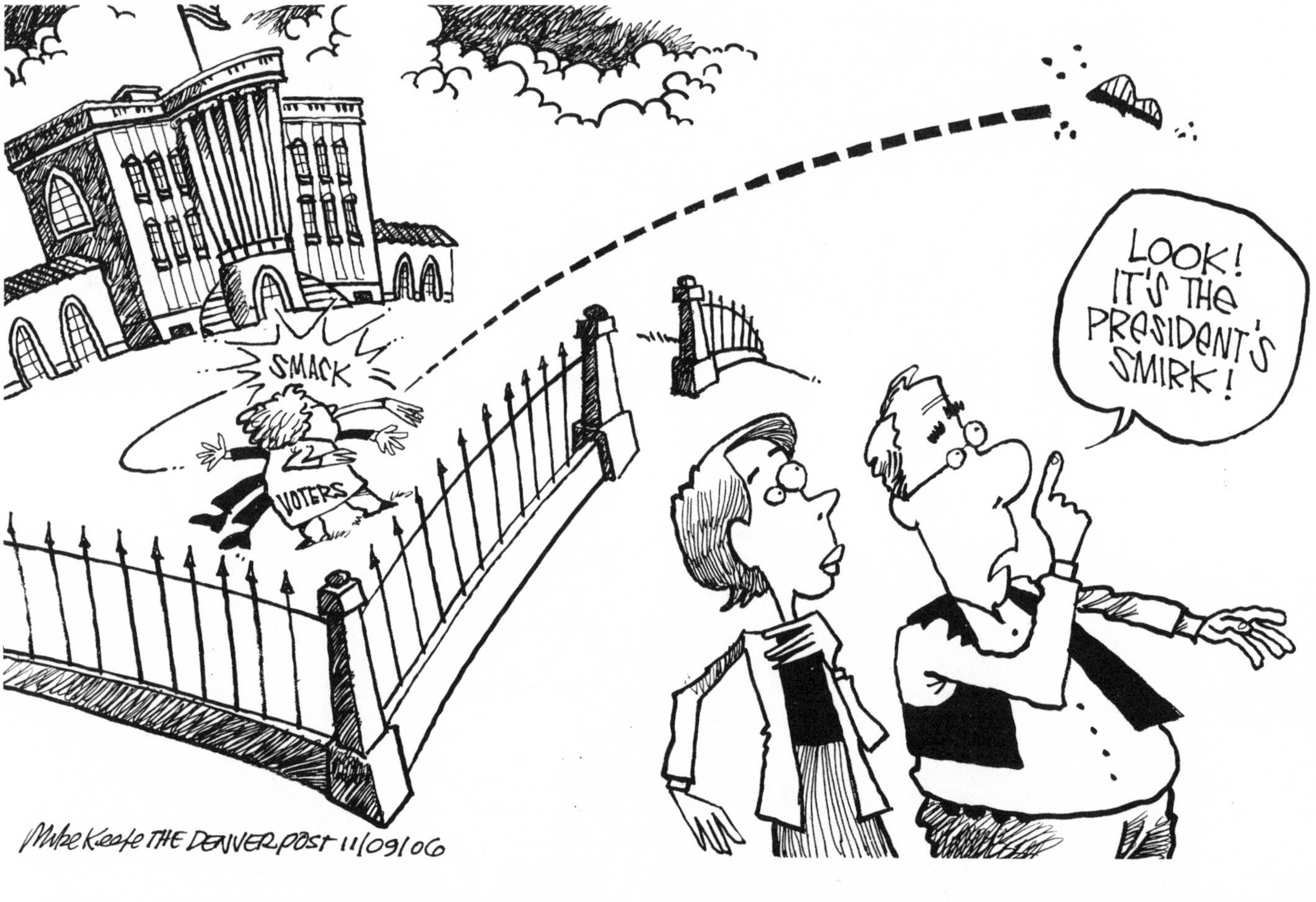
SMACK
VOTERS
LOOK! IT'S THE PRESIDENT'S SMIRK!
Mike Keefe THE DENVER POST 11/09/06

The November Elections

"It was a thumping," said President Bush in assessing the results of mid-term elections that handed the Democrats control of both houses of Congress. Democrats needed to pick up a net fifteen House seats and six Senate seats to wrest control from the GOP, who had controlled Congress since 1994. They easily captured the House and gained exactly six Senate seats to build a 51-49 majority. Many observers called it one of the nastiest campaigns in years, with particularly outrageous television ads tainting races in Missouri, and Ohio, and Georgia, and . . . well, a lot of other states.

The sobering loss was attributed to a variety of factors: GOP scandals, an unpopular war, and the historical tendency for the party in power to suffer significant losses in mid-term elections. Probable Republican presidential candidate Sen. John McCain offered his analysis: Too many Republicans had not been "careful stewards of taxpayers' dollars" and had not "adhered to conservative principles."

The ballots were still being counted when President Bush announced the resignation of embattled Defense Secretary Donald Rumsfeld. Former CIA Director Robert Gates, called by Bush "an agent of change," was named to replace him.

CLAY BENNETT
Courtesy Christian Science Monitor

THE CHRISTIAN SCIENCE MONITOR Bennett

THIS CAMPAIGN HAS BEEN A SHAMELESS EMBARRASSMENT!

'I'm an American voter and I approve this message.'

BOB GORRELL
Courtesy Creators Syndicate

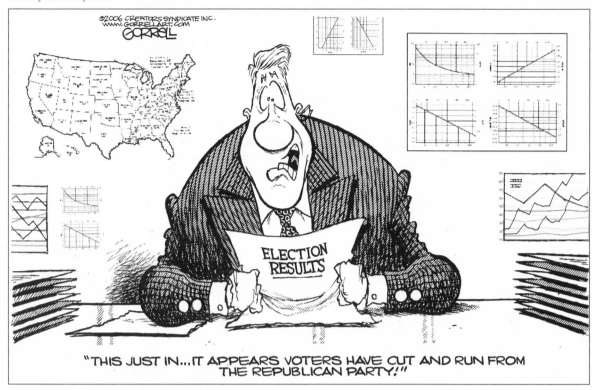

STEVE GREENBERG
Courtesy Ventura County Star

ED HALL
Courtesy DBR Media

MIKE PETERS
Courtesy Dayton Daily News

ED STEIN
Courtesy Rocky Mountain News (Colo.)

JAMES D. CROWE
Courtesy Mobile Register

Terrorism / Iraq

Worldwide terrorism showed no signs of lessening during 2006. Seven men, five of them United States citizens, were arrested in a plot to bomb the Sears Tower in Chicago. British authorities thwarted a plot to simultaneously blow up ten or more aircraft leaving London's Heathrow Airport. The terrorists intended to use explosives disguised as harmless liquids or gels. A plan to attack train tunnels around New York City was also defused.

The new government in Iraq seemed unable to make Baghdad and other parts of the country safe, even with the help of U.S. soldiers. Insurgents killed an average of scores of civilians a day throughout the year, primarily by suicide bombers and roadside explosive devices.

In Afghanistan, the Taliban increased the tempo of its attacks against the government. Troops from the U.S., Great Britain, and Canada continued to aid Afghani soldiers in their offensives against militant strongholds.

Zacarias Moussaoui, the only person to be tried in connection with the 9/11 terrorist attacks in New York, was found guilty and sentenced to life in prison. Abu Musab al-Zarqawi, the most wanted terrorist in Iraq, died when U.S. planes bombed his safehouse.

NICK ANDERSON
Courtesy Houston Chronicle

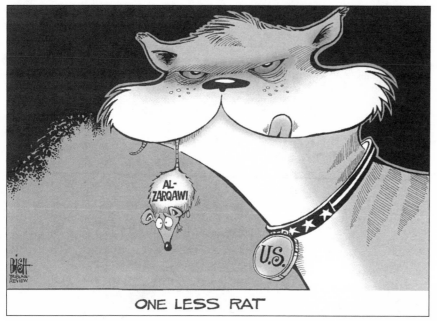

RANDY BISH
Courtesy Tribune-Review (Pa.)

JACK CHAPMAN
Courtesy DeSoto Times Today

ANN WHITNEY CLEAVES
Courtesy The Palisadian Post (Calif.)

STEVE BREEN
Courtesy San Diego Union-Tribune

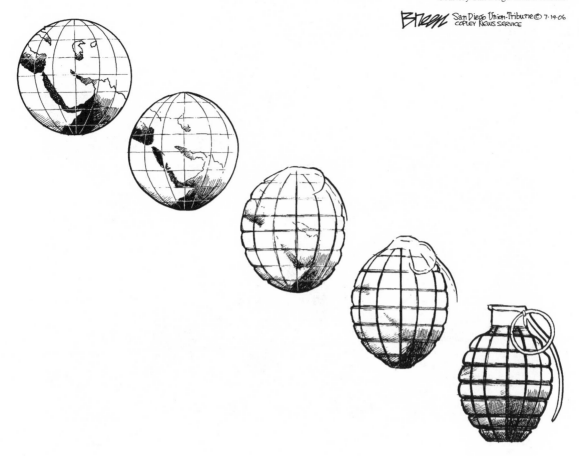

JAKE FULLER
Courtesy Gainesville Sun

THE MODERATE MUSLIM RESPONSE TO ISLAMIC TERRORISTS

SOMEWHERE IN SUBTERRANEAN PAKISTAN...

HAP PITKIN
Courtesy Boulder Daily Camera

JACK HIGGINS
Courtesy Chicago Sun-Times

CARL MOORE
Courtesy Creators Syndicate

SCOTT STANTIS
Courtesy Birmingham News

BRUCE BEATTIE
Courtesy Daytona Beach News-Journal

"He needs more matches to play with."

ROBERT ARIAIL
Courtesy The State (S.C.)

DAVID G. BROWN
Courtesy Los Angeles Sentinel

Prisoners who are confined and have little hope of being released soon...

Guantanamo

Iraq

Suspected terrorist

©2006 Rochester Post-Bulletin Co.L.L.C.
Ed Fischer Syndicate
fischer@postbulletin.com

U.S.

ED FISCHER

ED FISCHER
Courtesy Rochester Post-Bulletin

FIVE YEARS AFTER THE TOWERS FELL... FIVE YEARS AFTER— AND WAR'S STILL HELL.

FIVE YEARS AFTER AND NOT MUCH TO TELL... FIVE YEARS AFTER— OSAMA'S NOT IN A JAIL CELL.

AIRPORT SECURITY ABSOLUTELY NO LIQUIDS OR GELS

FIVE YEARS AFTER STILL WALKING ON EGGSHELLS... FIVE YEARS AFTER— GOD, I HOPE IT'S ABOUT MORE THAN OIL WELLS.

$65.70
19.4

Vitello

ALAN VITELLO
Courtesy Greeley Tribune

MARK BAKER
Courtesy Army Times

WILLIAM WALLACE
Courtesy Powell Tribune (Wyo.)

CLAY JONES
Courtesy Free Lance-Star (Va.)

WAYNE STAYSKAL
Courtesy Tribune Media Services

JERRY BARNETT
Courtesy Boonville Standard (Ind.)

ROY PETERSON
Courtesy Vancouver Sun

MARK BAKER
Courtesy Army Times

ED GAMBLE
Courtesy Florida Times-Union

ADAM ZYGLIS
Courtesy Buffalo News

BOB ENGLEHART
Courtesy Hartford Courant

STEVE GREENBERG
Courtesy Ventura County Star

ETTA HULME
Courtesy Fort Worth Star-Telegram

PIECE OF CAKE

ROB ROGERS
Courtesy Pittsburgh Post-Gazette

MARTY RISKIN
Courtesy Melrose Free Press (Mass.)

AARON TAYLOR
Courtesy The Daily Herald (Utah)

PAUL CONRAD
Courtesy Tribune Media Services

STEVE GREENBERG
Courtesy Ventura County Star

The Bush Administration

2006 was not a George Bush year.

First, he came under fire by Democrats over a National Security Agency program to eavesdrop on telephone conversations involving suspected al-Qaida agents. Critics called it unwarranted spying on citizens and a violation of civil rights. Then, administration plans to allow an Arab firm, Dubai Ports World, to operate six U.S. port terminals created another firestorm of controversy. The Arab company backed out of the deal because of the opposition. And finally, Democrats took control of Congress in the fall elections.

Vice President Dick Cheney accidentally shot a companion, attorney Harry Whittington, while quail hunting in Texas. Whittington made a full recovery.

Late in October Bush signed a law authorizing military trials for terrorist suspects. The legislation, bitterly attacked by the left wing, eliminated some defendant rights and approved harsh interrogation of terror suspects.

President Bush's approval ratings dipped into the 30s during 2006, apparently because of public dissatisfaction over the war in Iraq, the administration's slow response to Hurricane Katrina, and relentless attacks on the president by the Democrats and most of the media.

WALT HANDELSMAN
Courtesy Newsday

PAUL CONRAD
Courtesy Tribune Media Services

ROY PETERSON
Courtesy Vancouver Sun

JUSTIN DeFREITAS
Courtesy Berkeley Daily Planet

34

ROB ROGERS
Courtesy Pittsburgh Post-Gazette

JOHN SHERFFIUS
Courtesy Boulder Daily Camera

ROB HARRIMAN
Courtesy Portland Tribune

CHRIS BRITT
Courtesy State Journal-Register (Ill.)

STEVEN LAIT
Courtesy Oakland Tribune

HAP PITKIN
Courtesy Boulder Daily Camera

ETTA HULME
Courtesy Fort Worth Star-Telegram

ED STEIN
Courtesy Rocky Mountain News (Colo.)

CLAY BENNETT
Courtesy Christian Science Monitor

CHRIS BRITT
Courtesy State Journal-Register (Ill.)

ROB HARRIMAN
Courtesy Portland Tribune

JAMES CASCIARI
Courtesy Scripps Treasure Coast Newspapers

JIM BORGMAN
Courtesy Cincinnati Enquirer

" I HAVE BEEN INSTRUCTED BY MY CLIENTS, THE AMERICAN PEOPLE, TO EXTEND THIS VERY GENEROUS BUYOUT OFFER FOR THE FINAL 2½ YEARS OF YOUR CONTRACT.... WE DO HOPE YOU'LL CONSIDER IT. "

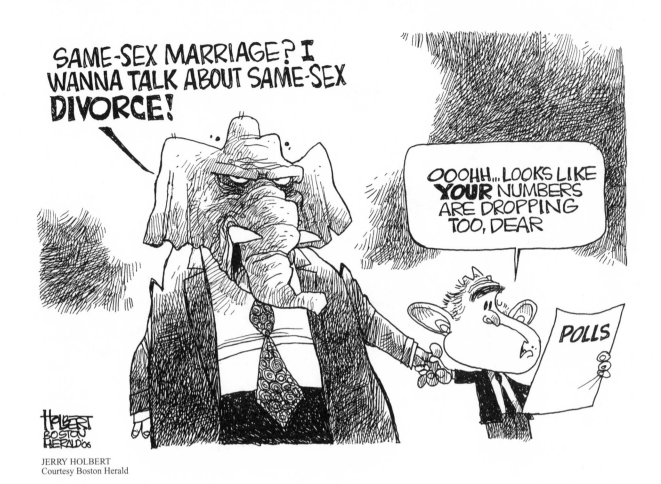

JERRY HOLBERT
Courtesy Boston Herald

PETER DUNLAP-SHOHL
Courtesy Anchorage Daily News

RICHARD WALLMEYER
Courtesy Long Beach Press-Telegram

GEORGE DANBY
Courtesy Bangor Daily News

MIKE KEEFE
Courtesy Denver Post

CHAN LOWE
Courtesy Fort Lauderdale News/Sun Sentinel

JOE HELLER
Courtesy Green Bay Press-Gazette

STAN BURDICK
Courtesy Lake Champlain Weekly (N.Y.)

ROB HARRIMAN
Courtesy Portland Tribune

CHARLIE HALL
Courtesy Rhode Island News Group

JACK HIGGINS
Courtesy Chicago Sun-Times

STEPHEN TEMPLETON
Courtesy The Observer-Times (Pa.)

GEORGE DANBY
Courtesy Bangor Daily News

STEVE KELLEY
Courtesy The Times-Picayune (La.)

JUSTIN DeFREITAS
Courtesy Berkeley Daily Planet

CHRIS BRITT
Courtesy State Journal-Register (Ill.)

MICHAEL THOMPSON
Courtesy Detroit Free Press

JIM BORGMAN
Courtesy Cincinnati Enquirer

LARRY WRIGHT
Courtesy Detroit News

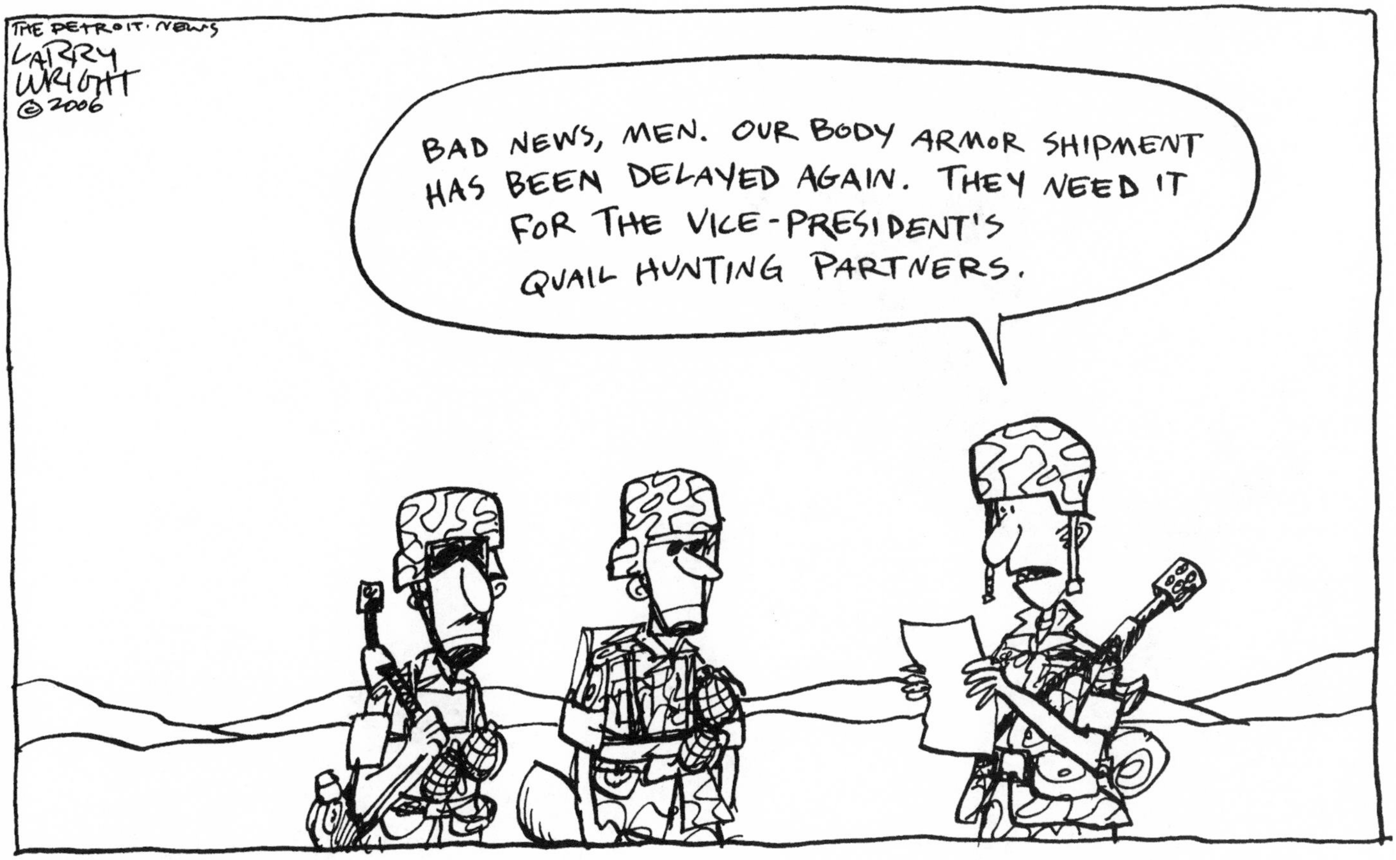
THE DETROIT NEWS
LARRY WRIGHT
© 2006
BAD NEWS, MEN. OUR BODY ARMOR SHIPMENT HAS BEEN DELAYED AGAIN. THEY NEED IT FOR THE VICE-PRESIDENT'S QUAIL HUNTING PARTNERS.

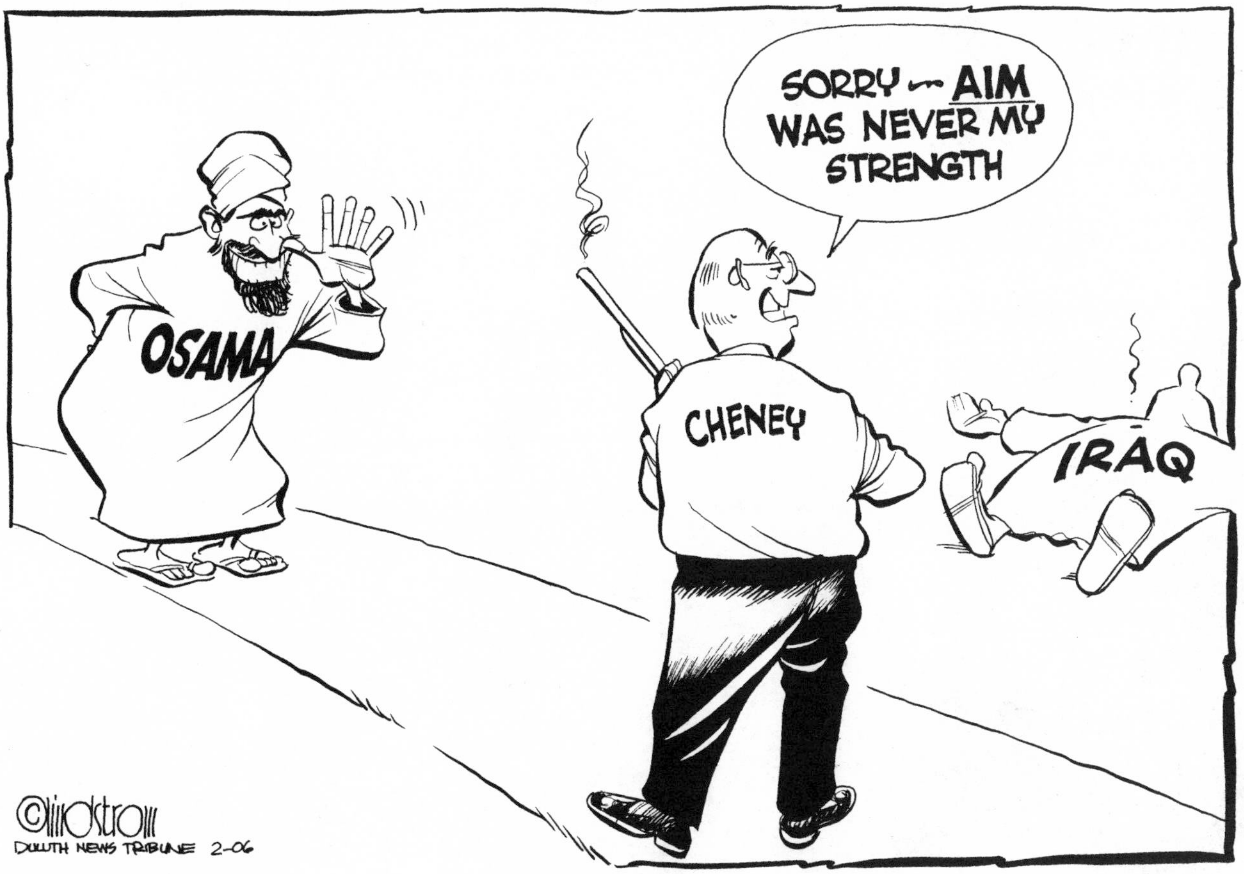
SORRY — AIM WAS NEVER MY STRENGTH
OSAMA
CHENEY
IRAQ
©LINDSTROM
DULUTH NEWS TRIBUNE 2-06

STEVE LINDSTROM
Courtesy Duluth News-Tribune

MIKE LUCKOVICH
Courtesy Atlanta Journal-Constitution

PAUL CONRAD
Courtesy Tribune Media Services

WALT HANDELSMAN
Courtesy Newsday

STEVE SACK
Courtesy Minneapolis Star-Tribune

RICHARD B. CROWSON
Courtesy Wichita Eagle

WALT HANDELSMAN
Courtesy Newsday

DAN CARINO
Courtesy Knight-Ridder/Tribune Information Services

JOE R. LANE
Courtesy Denton Record-Chronicle (Tex.)

JESSE SPRINGER
Courtesy Eugene Register-Guard (Ore.)

WALT HANDELSMAN
Courtesy Newsday

Bowing to criticism, the President decides to tone down interrogation tactics.

STEVE EDWARDS
Courtesy St. Louis Journalism Review

CHARLIE HALL
Courtesy Rhode Island News Group

ALAN J. NASH
Courtesy Gering Courier/North Platte Bulletin

JEFF PARKER
Courtesy Florida Today

CHRIS WRIGHT
Courtesy Bobwright@msn.com

TOM BECK
Courtesy Freeport Journal-Standard (Ill.)

MICHAEL THOMPSON
Courtesy Detroit Free Press

NICK ANDERSON
Courtesy Houston Chronicle

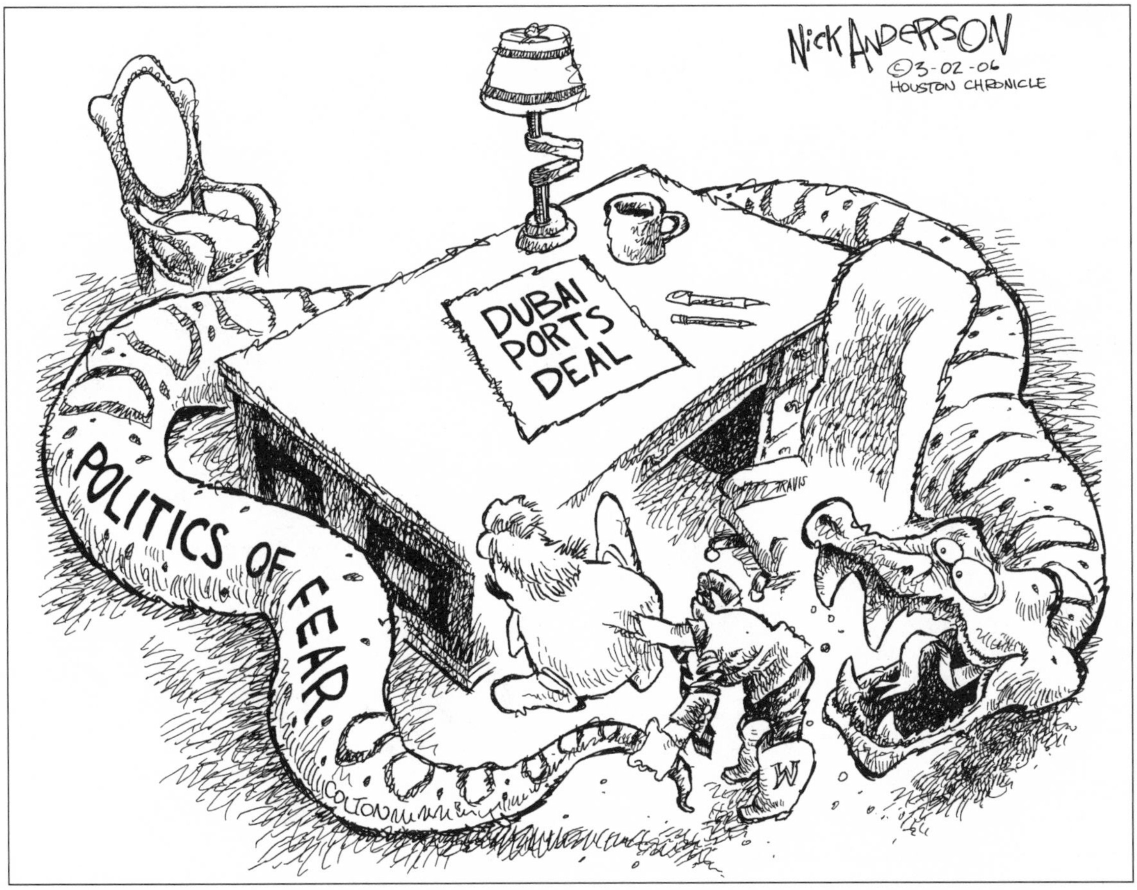

Nick Anderson
©3-02-06
Houston Chronicle
DUBAI PORTS DEAL
POLITICS OF FEAR

FRANK CAMMUSO
Courtesy The Post Standard

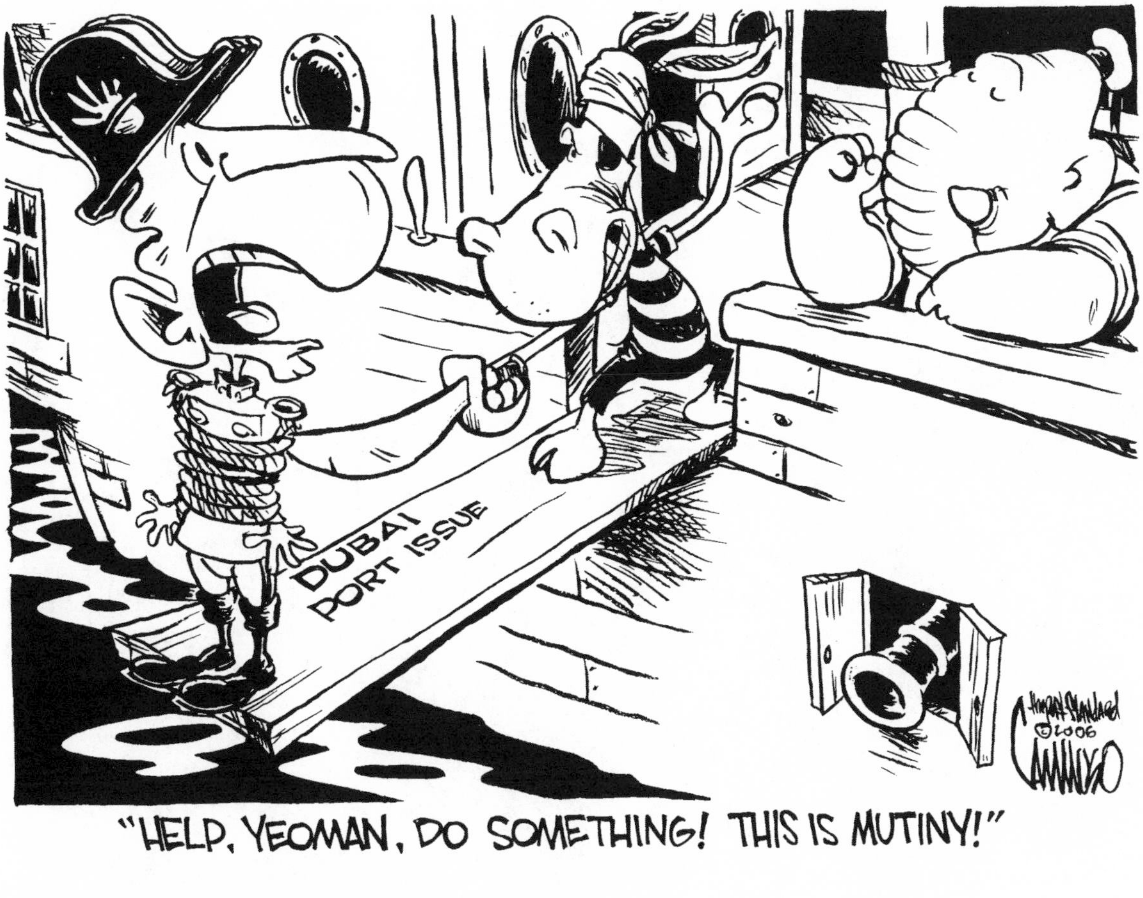

DUBAI PORT ISSUE
©2006
CAMMUSO

"HELP, YEOMAN, DO SOMETHING! THIS IS MUTINY!"

MIKE BECKOM
Courtesy Hartsville Messenger (S.C.)

MIKE KEEFE
Courtesy Denver Post

Immigration

There was much talk and little action by Congress on immigration reform during the year as thousands of illegal aliens continued to pour across the southern border into the U.S. A record 415 died in the attempt. It is estimated that some 12 million people reside illegally in the U.S.

Texas state officials began cracking down on criminals and suspected terrorists who attempted to cross the border. President Bush promoted a guest worker program that would allow illegals to stay in the country temporarily. His proposal met stiff opposition in his own party.

There was some slight movement on the part of Congress on the immigration issue. Legislation was passed to construct 700 miles of fence along the 2,000-mile U.S.-Mexican border. Priority was to be given to the area around Laredo, Texas, where warring drug cartels were blamed for more than 140 killings during the year.

Immigration reformers generally divided into two camps: those who oppose any sort of amnesty for illegal aliens, and those who want to provide a means for people already living in the U.S. illegally to become legal residents. On this issue there appeared to be little prospect for compromise.

WAYNE STROOT
Courtesy Hastings Tribune

ADAM ZYGLIS
Courtesy Buffalo News

RICKY NOBILE
Courtesy Hattiesburg American

ROBERT ARIAIL
Courtesy The State (S.C.)

"IF THE AMERICAN DREAM IS FOR AMERICANS ONLY, IT WILL
REMAIN OUR DREAM AND NEVER BE OUR DESTINY."
~RENE DE VISME WILLIAMSON

TOM STIGLICH
Courtesy Northeast Times (Pa.)

ALAN J. NASH
Courtesy Gering Courier/North Platte Bulletin

IRENE JOSLIN
Courtesy The Republic (Ind.)

JIM BUSH
Courtesy Providence Journal (R.I.)

JEFF STAHLER
Courtesy Columbus Dispatch

BOB GORRELL
Courtesy Creators Syndicate

DEB MILBRATH
Courtesy AAEC CNN

WAYNE STAYSKAL
Courtesy Tribune Media Services

JIM DYKE
Courtesy Jefferson City News-Tribune

DICK LOCHER
Courtesy Chicago Tribune

JERRY BARNETT
Courtesy Boonville Standard (Ind.)

TONY BAYER
Courtesy The News-Dispatch (Ind.)

MIKE LESTER
Courtesy Rome News-Tribune (Ga.)

JIM HOPE
Courtesy Culpepper Star-Exponent (Va.)

POL GALVEZ
Courtesy Philippine News (Calif.)

JOHN GUTEKUNST
Courtesy Parker Pioneer (Ariz.)

HAP PITKIN
Courtesy Boulder Daily Camera

STEVE KELLEY
Courtesy The Times-Picayune (La.)

JOE HELLER
Courtesy Green Bay Press-Gazette

PAUL FELL
Courtesy Lincoln Journal Star

MIKE LUCKOVICH
Courtesy Atlanta Journal-Constitution

JOSEPH RANK
Courtesy Times-Press Recorder (Calif.)

REX BABIN
Courtesy Sacramento Bee

Senate-Approved Interrogation Techniques

GARY VARVEL
Courtesy Indianapolis Star

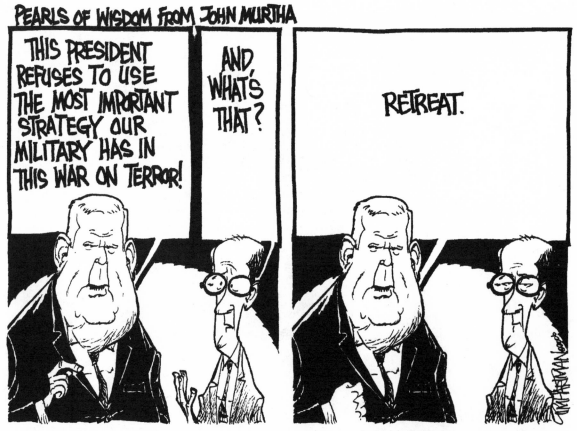

TIM HARTMAN
Courtesy Beaver County Times-Record (Pa.)

Congress

Scandals tarnished the congressional image of the dominant Republican Party during 2006. Former majority leader Tom DeLay resigned following his indictment for alleged illegal use of funds for state legislative races. GOP Rep. Randy Cunningham was sentenced to eight years in prison for taking $2.4 million in bribes, and Rep. Bob Ney pleaded guilty in the Jack Abramoff influence-peddling investigation.

Then, in October, just before the congressional elections, Rep. Tom Foley, a Florida Republican, suddenly resigned in the wake of allegations he had sent salacious emails to teenage male pages working for other congressmen. Democrats claimed that House Speaker Dennis Hastert, a Republican, should have known about Foley's indiscretions and forced him to resign.

In October, Congress passed significant anti-terrorism legislation, authorizing military trials for terrorist suspects and approving aggressive interrogation methods. But Congress failed to deal with other major issues, including immigration, a national energy policy, and expanded health insurance coverage. On balance, the great deliberative body worked fewer days and probably accomplished less than any other Congress in recent history.

MIKE LUCKOVICH
Courtesy Atlanta Journal-Constitution

JIM HUNT
Courtesy Charlotte Post

FRANK PAGE
Courtesy Rome Daily Sentinel (N.Y.)

FRANK CAMMUSO
Courtesy The Post Standard

JAKE FULLER
Courtesy Gainesville Sun

CLAY BENNETT
Courtesy Christian Science Monitor

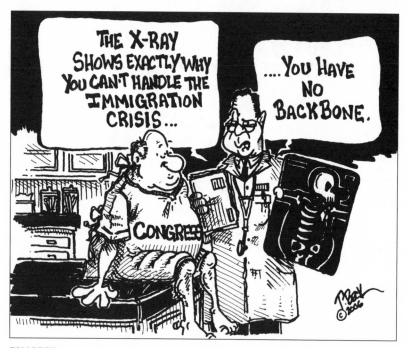

TOM BECK
Courtesy Freeport Journal-Standard (Ill.)

PAUL COMBS
Courtesy Tampa Tribune

LARRY WRIGHT
Courtesy Detroit News

SCOTT STANTIS
Courtesy Birmingham News

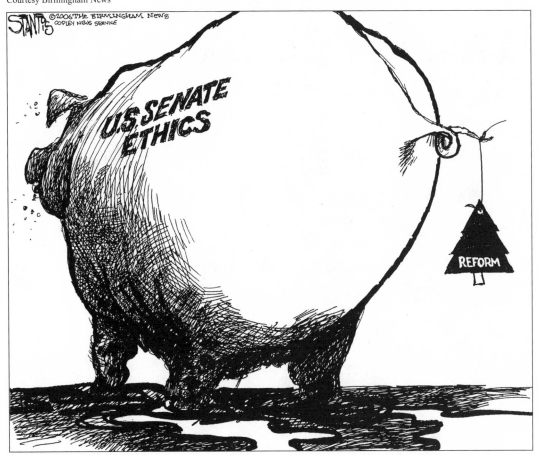

GARY MARKSTEIN
Courtesy Copley News Service

TOM BECK
Courtesy Freeport Journal-Standard (Ill.)

STEVE LINDSTROM
Courtesy Duluth News-Tribune

Foreign Affairs

The kidnapping of two Israeli soldiers ignited a major conflict against the terrorist group Hezbollah in Lebanon, with Israel carrying out massive air strikes and Hezbollah firing thousands of rockets against Israeli cities. The entrenched terrorists had dug elaborate tunnels and stockpiled massive caches of weapons from Iran and Syria under the eyes of a United Nations peacekeeping force. Mounting civilian casualties eventually led to a tenuous ceasefire.

A defiant North Korea announced the test of a small nuclear device, prompting world condemnation and raising the threat of United Nations sanctions against the renegade nation. Earlier, the Koreans test-fired a long-range missile capable of reaching the U.S. but it failed seconds after launch.

Rape and murder continued to wrack the African nation of Darfur. A May peacekeeping agreement to aid the besieged country collapsed, and humanitarian assistance fell to its lowest level since 2004.

In Mexico, conservative Felipe Calderon defeated populist Andres Manuel Lopez Obrador by a narrow margin, eliciting claims of voter fraud and touching off widespread violence. In Cuba, Fidel Castro fell seriously ill and transferred temporary authority to his brother Raul. And Britain's Tony Blair announced he would retire in the coming months.

MICHAEL RAMIREZ
Courtesy Investor's Business Daily

PORTRAIT OF HITLER.... WITH AN ATOMIC BOMB

ED HALL
Courtesy DBR Media

TERRY C. WISE
Courtesy Ratland Ink Press

BOB ENGLEHART
Courtesy Hartford Courant

REX BABIN
Courtesy Sacramento Bee

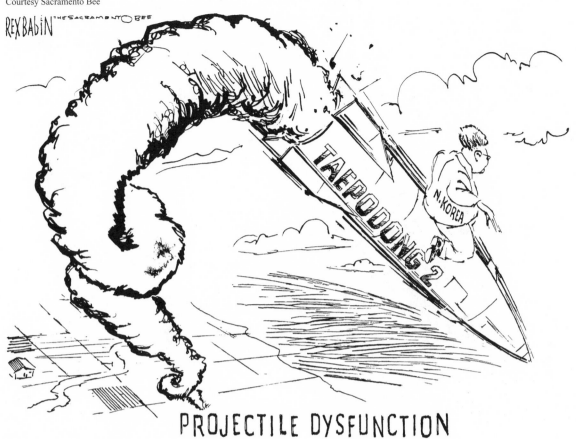

PROJECTILE DYSFUNCTION

AARON TAYLOR
Courtesy The Daily Herald (Utah)

REX BABIN
Courtesy Sacramento Bee

TIM JACKSON
Courtesy Chicago Defender

STEVE McBRIDE
Courtesy Independence Daily Reporter (Kan.)

Prime Minister Blair Blasted by Families of British Troops in Iraq

JEFF DANZIGER
Courtesy NYTS/CWS

JEFF STAHLER
Courtesy Columbus Dispatch

LINDA BOILEAU
Courtesy Frankfort State Journal (Ky.)

DICK LOCHER
Courtesy Chicago Tribune

PAUL NOWAK
Courtesy Scripps-Howard Service

GARY VARVEL
Courtesy Indianapolis Star

MICHAEL THOMPSON
Courtesy Detroit Free Press

CLAY BENNETT
Courtesy Christian Science Monitor

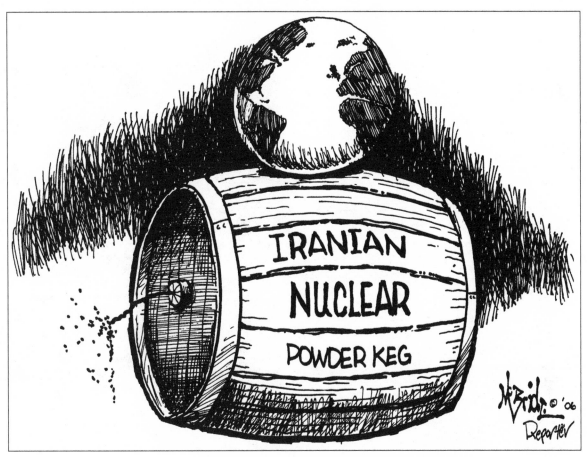

STEVE McBRIDE
Courtesy Independence Daily Reporter (Kan.)

JERRY HOLBERT
Courtesy Boston Herald

87

CHANCE of PEACE in the MIDDLE EAST

MIX WELL...

WATER

OIL

LINDA BOILEAU
Courtesy Frankfort State Journal (Ky.)

GUY BADEAUX
Courtesy Le Droit (Canada)

THE MORE THINGS CHANGE...

SEPTEMBER 1938

SEPTEMBER 2006

Neville

Kofi

DEAN P. TURNBLOOM
Courtesy USA Today

DAVID HITCH
Courtesy Worcester Telegram and Gazette (Mass.)

JAMES McCLOSKEY
Courtesy The News-Leader (Va.)

JACK JURDEN
Courtesy Wilmington News Journal

GARY MARKSTEIN
Courtesy Copley News Service

TOM STIGLICH
Courtesy Northeast Times (Pa.)

DAVID DONAR
Courtesy Macomb Daily (Miss.)

HAP PITKIN
Courtesy Boulder Daily Camera

GUY BADEAUX
Courtesy Le Droit (Canada)

PEDRO MOLINA
Courtesy El Nuevo Diario

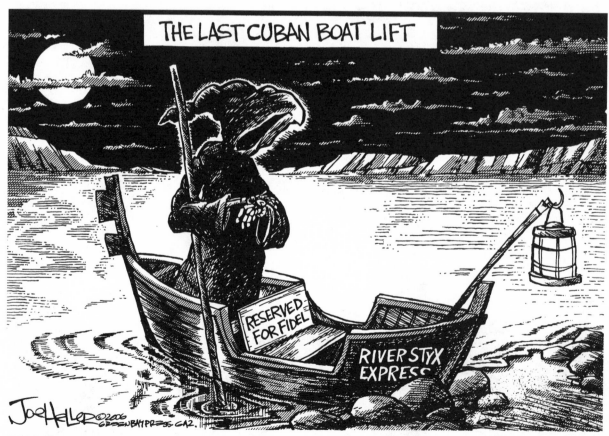

JOE HELLER
Courtesy Green Bay Press-Gazette

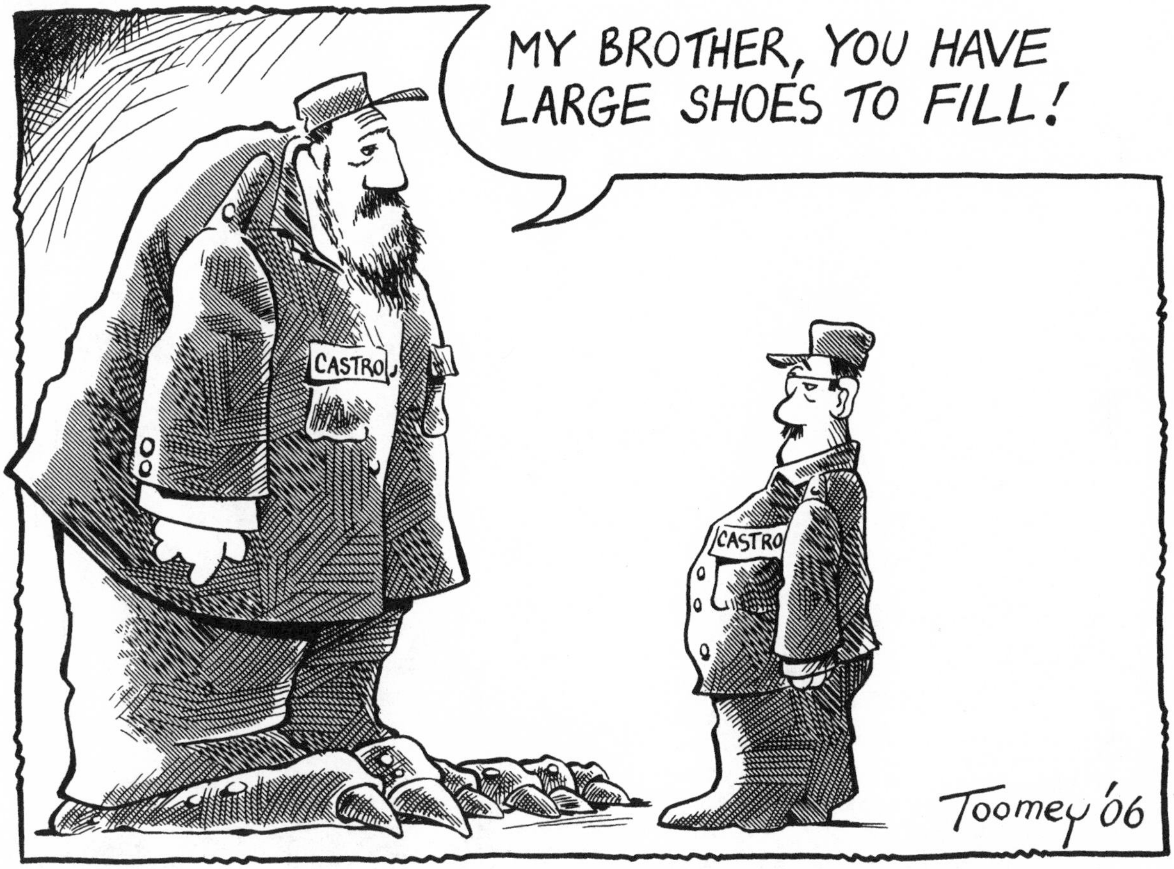
MY BROTHER, YOU HAVE LARGE SHOES TO FILL!
CASTRO
CASTRO
Toomey '06

MARSHALL TOOMEY
Courtesy Santa Clarita Signal (Calif.)

LARRY WRIGHT
Courtesy Detroit News

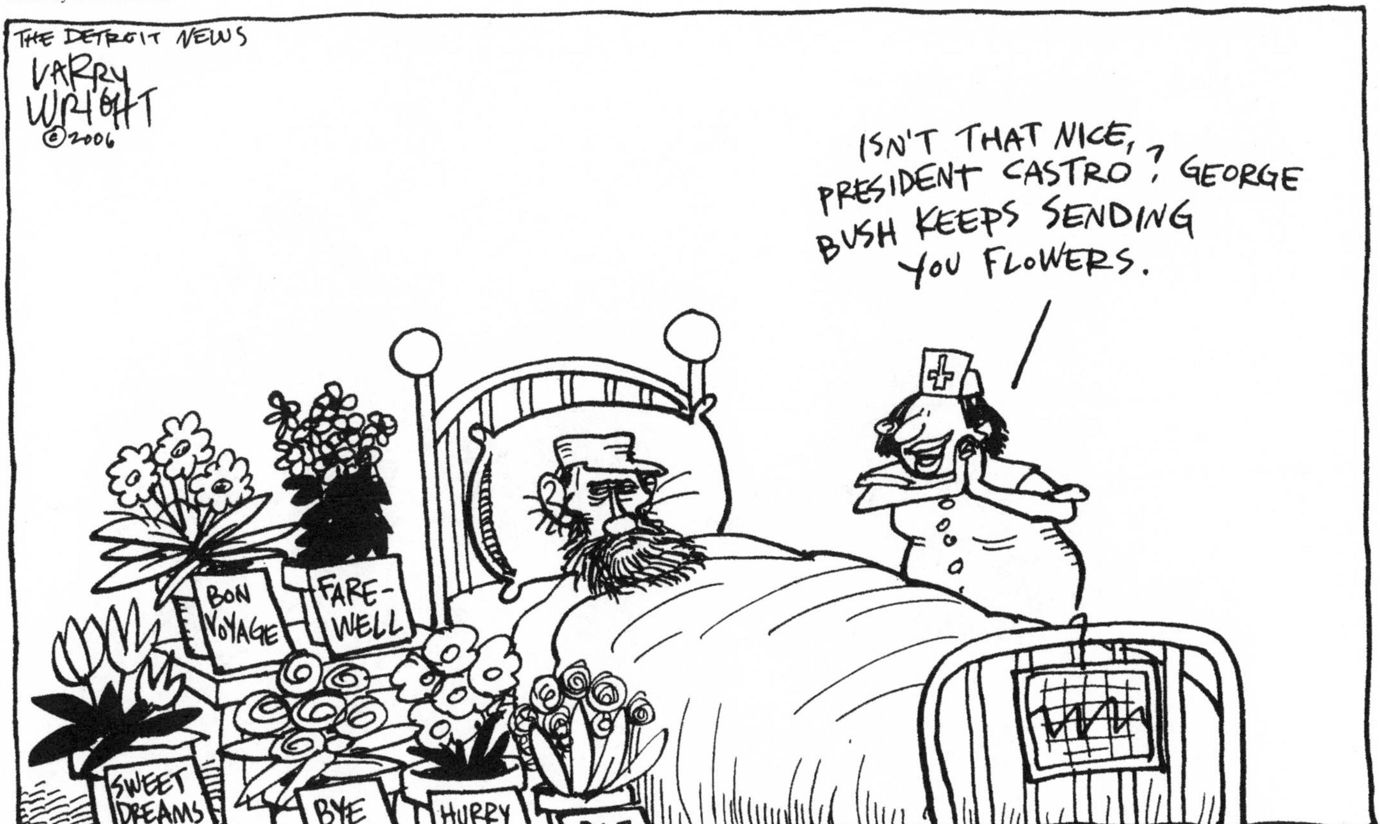
THE DETROIT NEWS
LARRY WRIGHT ©2006
ISN'T THAT NICE, PRESIDENT CASTRO? GEORGE BUSH KEEPS SENDING YOU FLOWERS.
BON VOYAGE
FARE-WELL
SWEET DREAMS
BYE
HURRY

FRANK PAGE
Courtesy Rome Daily Sentinel (N.Y.)

ADAM ZYGLIS
Courtesy Buffalo News

ETTA HULME
Courtesy Fort Worth Star-Telegram

ED GAMBLE
Courtesy Florida Times-Union

95

BOB GORRELL
Courtesy Creators Syndicate

JIMMY MARGULIES
Courtesy The Record (N.J.)

BOB GORRELL
Courtesy Creators Syndicate

TONY BAYER
Courtesy The News-Dispatch (Ind.)

MICHAEL RAMIREZ
Courtesy Investor's Business Daily

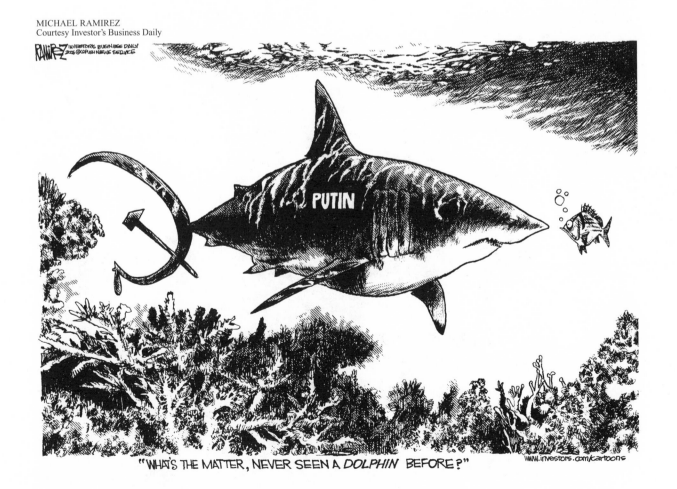

97

GARY MARKSTEIN
Courtesy Copley News Service

JEFF DANZIGER
Courtesy NYTS/CWS

Politics

Intra-party politics almost toppled a party icon. In Connecticut, veteran Sen. Joseph Lieberman, a staunch supporter of the war in Iraq, was defeated by political newcomer Ned Lamont in the Democratic primary. It was rough treatment, indeed, for Lieberman, widely regarded as a model mainstream Democrat on every issue except the war, to be rejected by his own party.

The former Democratic vice presidential candidate ultimately prevailed, however. Running again in the general election as an independent and attracting strong support from Republican voters, he overcame the opposition of party leaders and won handily.

Going into the election, surveys showed a powerful anti-incumbent mood and dissatisfaction with President Bush over a lack of progress in the war in Iraq. Coupled with allegations of scandal involving several GOP congressmen and widespread unhappiness over unrestrained Republican spending, it all seemed to set the stage for a political realignment in Washington.

Democrats had loudly criticized the Bush Administration's monitoring of telephone calls involving suspected terrorists, but dropped the issue when poll after poll showed strong public support for anti-terrorist surveillance.

ROBERT ARIAIL
Courtesy The State (S.C.)

RUSSELL HODIN
Courtesy New Times (Calif.)

JIM LANGE
Courtesy Daily Oklahoman

AARON TAYLOR
Courtesy The Daily Herald (Utah)

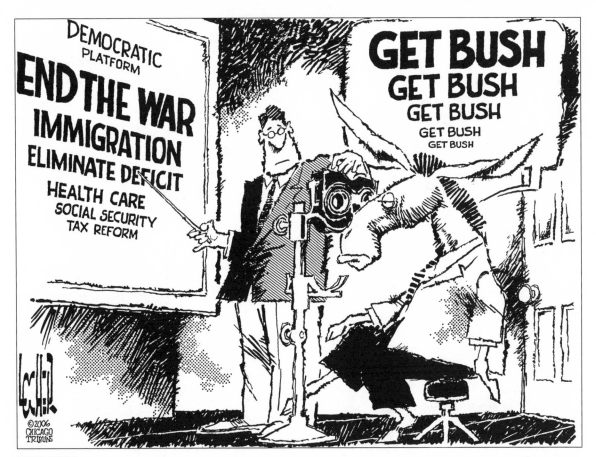

DICK LOCHER
Courtesy Chicago Tribune

ROBERT ARIAIL
Courtesy The State (S.C.)

JOHN BRANCH
Courtesy San Antonio Express-News

WILLIAM FLINT
Courtesy Dallas Morning News

DOUGLAS REGALIA
Courtesy Contra Costa Newspaper Group

JOHN SHERFFIUS
Courtesy Boulder Daily Camera

JOEL THORNHILL
Courtesy Lawrence County Record

RICHARD WALLMEYER
Courtesy Long Beach Press-Telegram

CHUCK ASAY
Courtesy Colorado Springs
Gazette-Telegraph

DAVID HITCH
Courtesy Worcester Telegram and Gazette (Mass.)

MIKE LUCKOVICH
Courtesy Atlanta Journal-Constitution

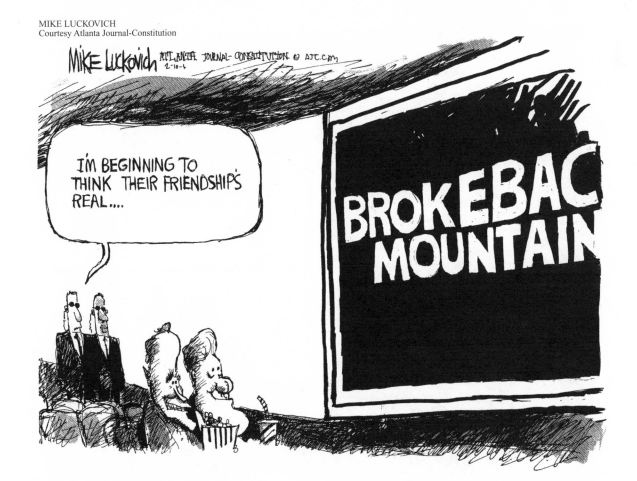

JOHN RILEY
Courtesy Johnrileycartoons.com

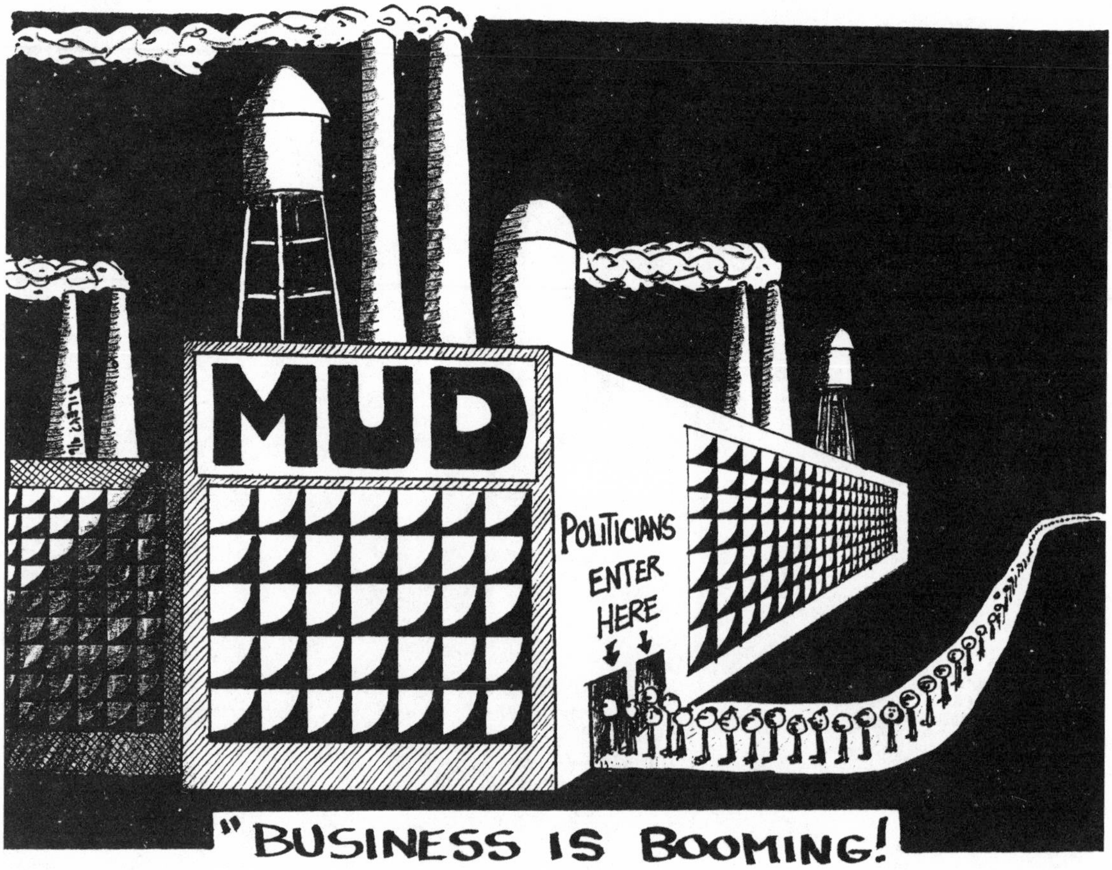
MUD
POLITICIANS ENTER HERE
"BUSINESS IS BOOMING!

STEVE KELLEY
Courtesy The Times-Picayune (La.)

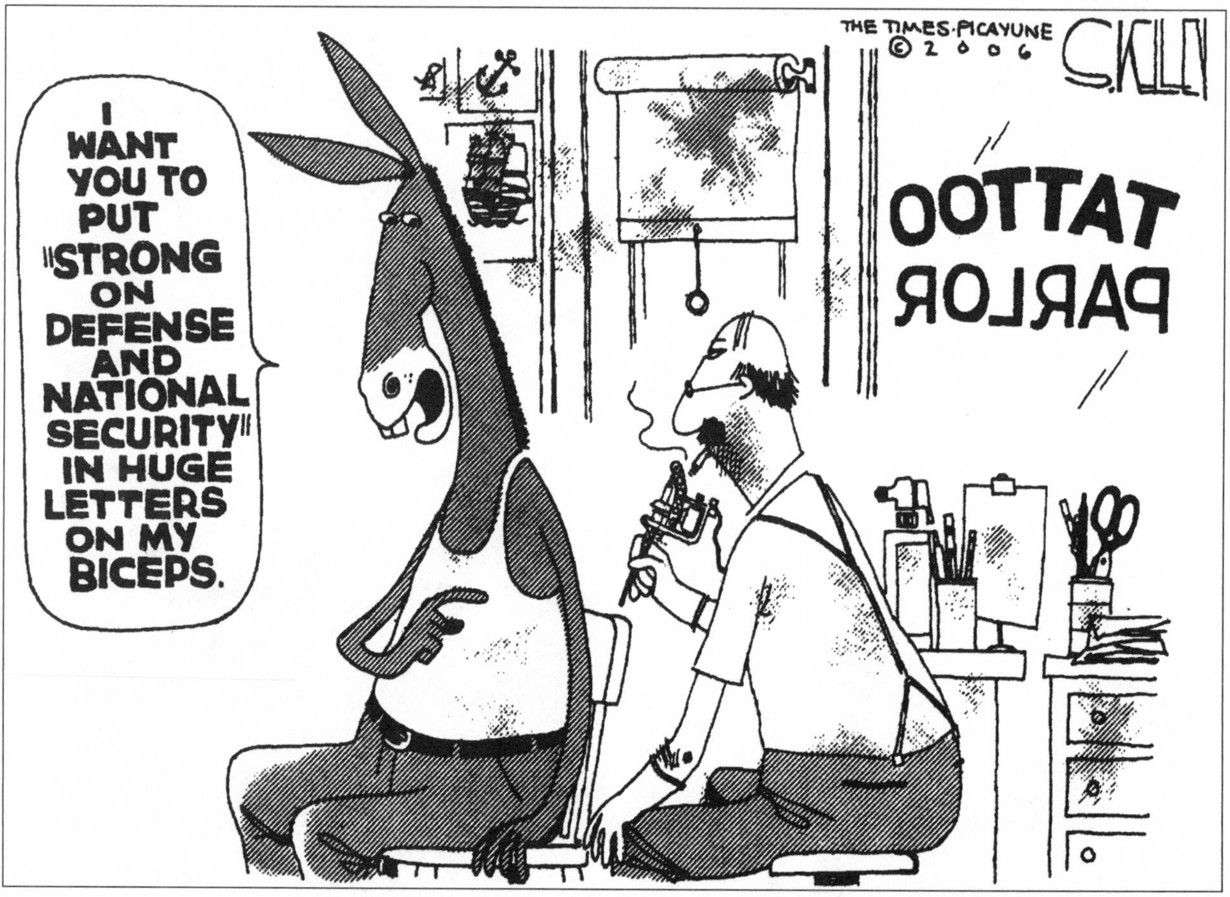
THE TIMES-PICAYUNE ©2006
S.KELLEY
I WANT YOU TO PUT "STRONG ON DEFENSE AND NATIONAL SECURITY" IN HUGE LETTERS ON MY BICEPS.
OOTTAT PARLOR

CHUCK ASAY
Courtesy Colorado Springs
  Gazette-Telegraph

The Republican Revolution

NICK ANDERSON
Courtesy Houston Chronicle

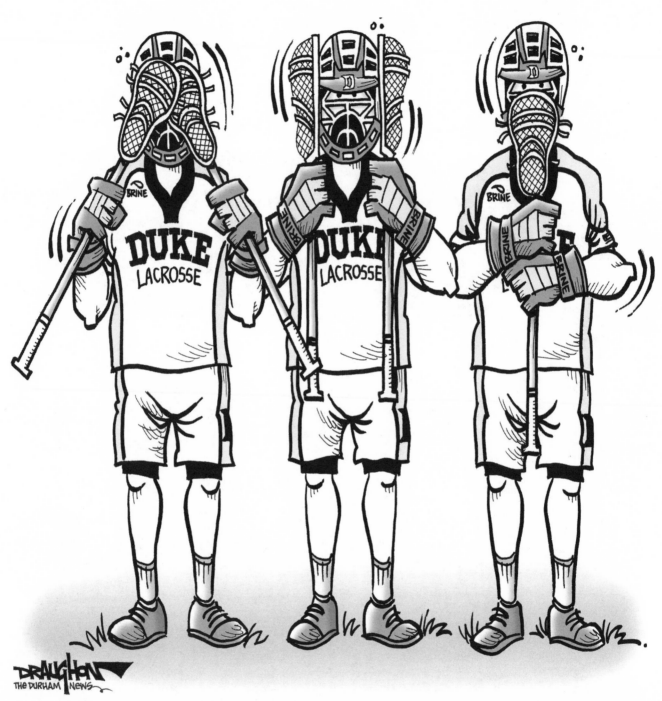

DENNIS DRAUGHON
Courtesy Durham News

Crime

Former Enron Corporation executives Kenneth Lay and Jeffrey Skilling were convicted of conspiracy to commit securities and wire fraud in one of the biggest cases of corporate wrongdoing in American history. Lay died a few weeks later with the case still on appeal. Jack Abramoff, the lobbyist who spawned a potentially far-reaching congressional probe, pleaded guilty to three felonies and promised to cooperate with investigators.

Prosecutors in the decade-old slaying of JonBenet Ramsey arrested Alabama native John Mark Karr, who had implicated himself in the crime, but DNA tests exonerated him.

Three college students were accused of setting a string of nine church fires across Alabama. Federal agents said the defendants claimed the first few blazes were set "as a joke." Members of the Duke University lacrosse team were accused of raping an exotic dancer hired to perform at a party, but evidence appeared to be lacking.

Violent crime in America edged up in 2006 by 2.5 percent after several years of decline. Cities with populations of between 500,000 and one million recorded the biggest increase, 8.3 percent. Murders and manslaughter jumped 4.8 percent.

DOUGLAS REGALIA
Courtesy Contra Costa Newspaper Group

MIKE PETERS
Courtesy Dayton Daily News

RUSSELL HODIN
Courtesy New Times (Calif.

WAYNE STAYSKAL
Courtesy Tribune Media Services

JACK HIGGINS
Courtesy Chicago Sun-Times

STEVE SACK
Courtesy Minneapolis Star-Tribune

DANA SUMMERS
Courtesy Orlando Sentinel

CLAY JONES
Courtesy Free Lance-Star (Va.)

JAMES CASCIARI
Courtesy Scripps Treasure Coast Newspapers

ELENA STEIER
Courtesy The Valley News

MIKE PETERS
Courtesy Dayton Daily News

PAUL FELL
Courtesy Lincoln Journal Star

JONATHAN TODD
Courtesy Shreveport Times

Health / Environment

The Centers for Disease Control continued to warn that obesity remains one of America's biggest health problems. Some 20 percent of children are overweight, as are 65 percent of all adults. *The New England Journal of Medicine* reported that those who carry extra pounds into their fifties can expect a shorter life span.

The Federal Emergency Management Agency (FEMA) continued to generate criticism for its slow response in aiding recovery efforts after Hurricane Katrina. A great many victims were still waiting for grants to rebuild their homes more than a year later.

Early in the year, a stray cat in Germany died of bird flu, which has killed scores of people worldwide. Many Germans dumped their cats at the animal welfare society, and demand for poultry plummeted across Europe. An outbreak of E. coli led to the recall of packaged spinach from stores across North America.

The U.S. suffered from unusually dry weather during the year, reminding some very old timers of the Dust Bowl conditions of the 1930s. Temperatures in Great Britain, normally in the seventies in July, reached 100 degrees, and heat-related deaths were reported in the Netherlands, Spain, and France.

Stem cell research continued to stir controversy.

ETTA HULME
Courtesy Fort Worth Star-Telegram

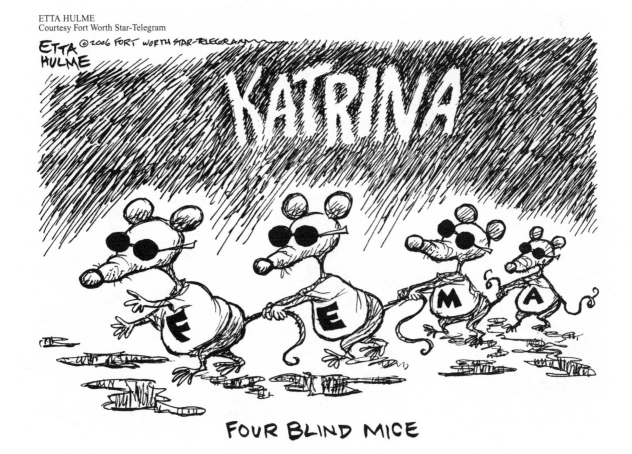

FOUR BLIND MICE

ELIZABETH BRICQUET
Courtesy Kingsport Times-News (Tenn.)

JAMES D. CROWE
Courtesy Mobile Register

SYBIL M. VETRA
Courtesy News-Journal (N.C.)

TIM HARTMAN
Courtesy Beaver County Times-Record (Pa.)

117

J. R. ROSE
Courtesy Byrd Newspapers/Daily News Record

MARK STREETER
Courtesy Savannah Morning News

RICHARD B. CROWSON
Courtesy Wichita Eagle

118

JERRY BARNETT
Courtesy Boonville Standard (Ind.)

STEVE SACK
Courtesy Minneapolis Star-Tribune

PETER K. EVANS
Courtesy Islander News (Fla.)

JEFF STAHLER
Courtesy Columbus Dispatch

BOB GORRELL
Courtesy Creators Syndicate

120

JAMES CASCIARI
Courtesy Scripps Treasure Coast Newspapers

DICK LOCHER
Courtesy Chicago Tribune

121

HAP PITKIN
Courtesy Boulder Daily Camera

CLAY BENNETT
Courtesy Christian Science Monitor

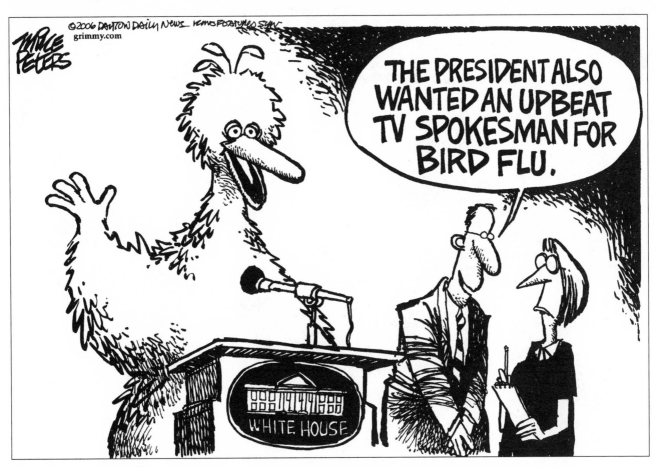

MIKE PETERS
Courtesy Dayton Daily News

WAYNE STAYSKAL
Courtesy Tribune Media Services

DANIEL FENECH
Courtesy Saline Reporter (Mich.)

DEB MILBRATH
Courtesy AAEC CNN

STEVE EDWARDS
Courtesy St. Louis Journalism Review

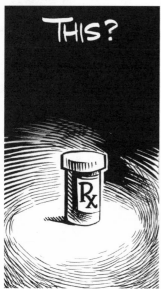

JAMES D. CROWE
Courtesy Mobile Register

NICK ANDERSON
Courtesy Houston Chronicle

BILL GARNER
Courtesy Washington Times

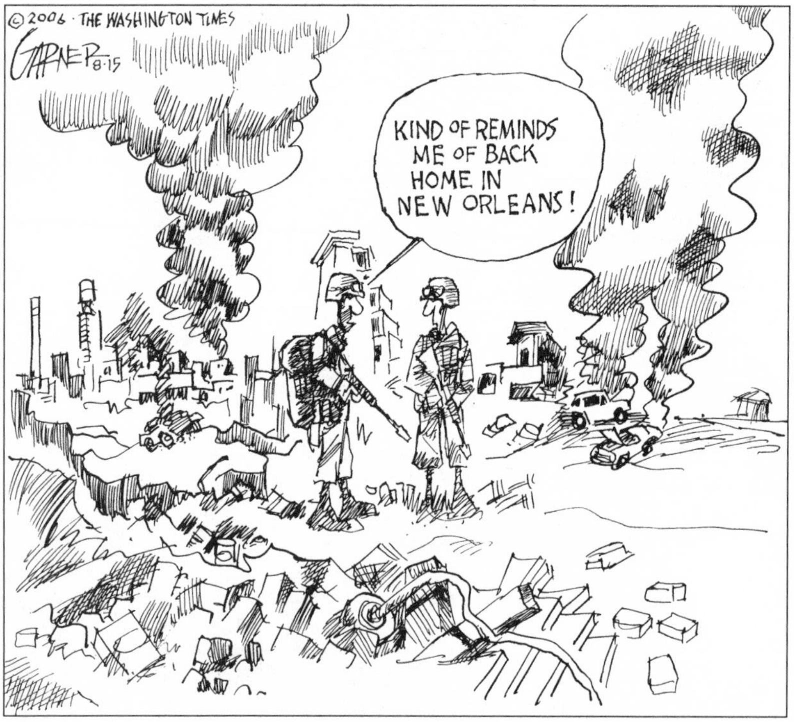
© 2006 · THE WASHINGTON TIMES
GARNER 8·15
KIND OF REMINDS ME OF BACK HOME IN NEW ORLEANS!

BOB WIEGERS
Courtesy Rockford Register-Star (Ill.)

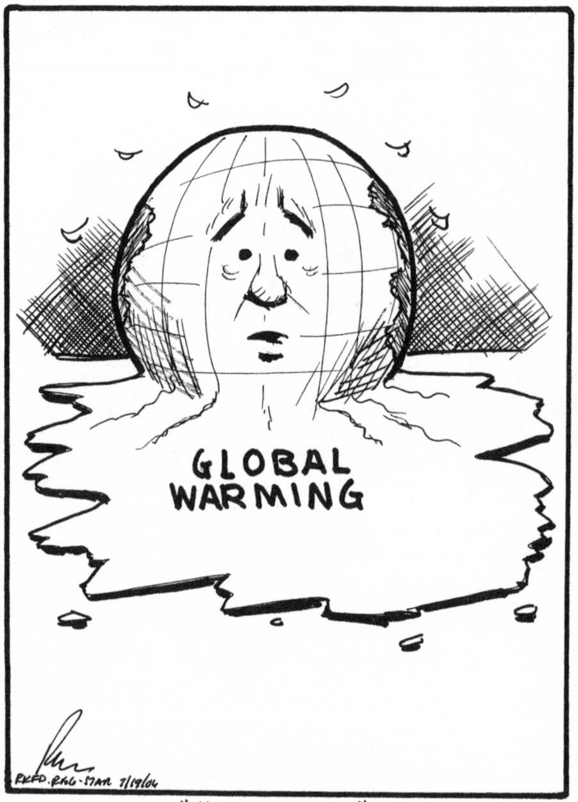
GLOBAL WARMING
RKFD. REG-STAR 7/19/06

"I'M MELTING"

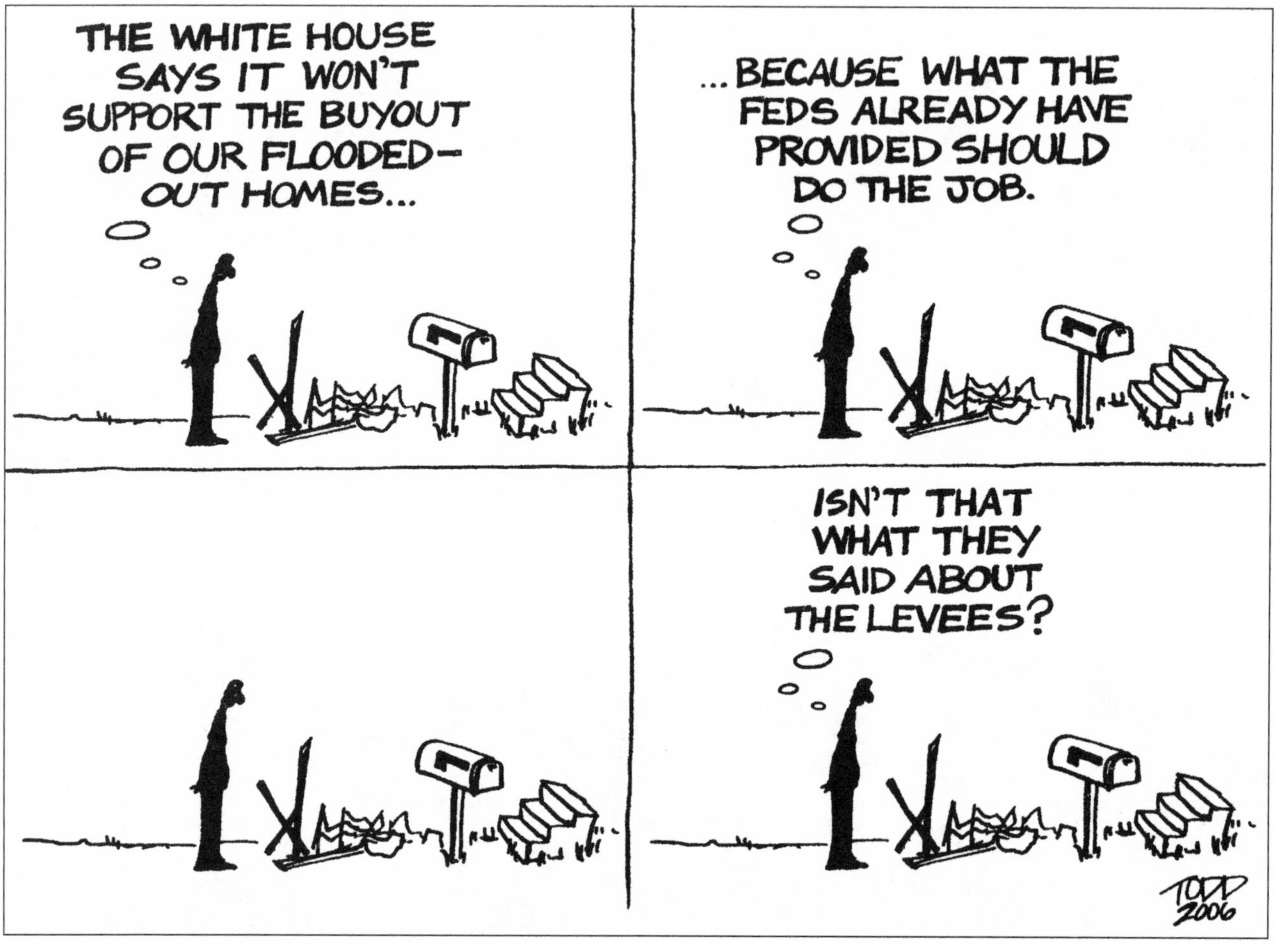
THE WHITE HOUSE SAYS IT WON'T SUPPORT THE BUYOUT OF OUR FLOODED-OUT HOMES...
...BECAUSE WHAT THE FEDS ALREADY HAVE PROVIDED SHOULD DO THE JOB.
ISN'T THAT WHAT THEY SAID ABOUT THE LEVEES?
TODD 2006

JONATHAN TODD
Courtesy Shreveport Times

ED FISCHER
Courtesy Rochester Post-Bulletin

JOE HELLER
Courtesy Green Bay Press-Gazette

JOEL PETT
Courtesy Lexington Herald-Leader

GENE HERNDON
Courtesy Noblesville Daily Times (Ind.)

"We have to put you on a diet, Johnny. The doctors say you're obese."

JIMMY MARGULIES
Courtesy The Record (N.J.)

WILL O'TOOLE
Courtesy Home News and Tribune (N.J.)

DENNIS DRAUGHON
Courtesy Durham New[s]

PAUL COMBS
Courtesy Tampa Tribune

Sports

Barry Bonds of the San Francisco Giants eclipsed the immortal Babe Ruth's lifetime total of 714 homeruns and ended the season with a total of 724. Hank Aaron, however, still holds the all-time major league record of 755 home runs. Bonds also tied Willie Mays' all-time record of 1,903 runs batted in.

A shadow of suspicion, however, clouds the Bonds achievement following accusations of steroid use. Until a few years ago it was legal to use certain performance-enhancing drugs, including steroids. Major league baseball has been grappling with the problems associated with the use of such drugs for several years now. One question the leagues must address is whether asterisks should be used to identify records believed to have been achieved with performance-enhancing drugs that are no longer legal.

Tennis star Andre Agassi's 20-year career ended in defeat at the hands of German qualifier Benjamin Becker at the U.S. Open. The 36-year-old was clearly affected by the chronic back problem that hastened his decision to retire.

The St. Louis Cardinals defeated the Detroit Tigers in five games to win the 2006 World Series.

ED HALL
Courtesy DBR Media

131

JAMES CASCIARI
Courtesy Scripps Treasure Coast Newspapers

GERALD L. GARDEN
Courtesy The UTP Voice (Calif.)

CHARLES DANIEL
Courtesy Knoxville News-Sentinel

MICHAEL RAMIREZ
Courtesy Investor's Business Daily

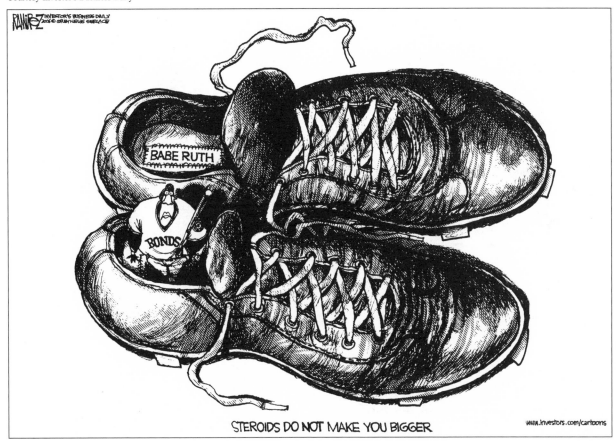

TOM STIGLICH
Courtesy Northeast Times (Pa.)

DAVID DONAR
Courtesy Macomb Daily (Miss.)

CHARLIE HALL
Courtesy Rhode Island News Group

JOE HOFFECKER
Courtesy Cincinnati Business Courier

Society

Warren Buffett, named by *Forbes* magazine as the world's second-richest man, donated 85 percent of his $42 billion fortune to the Bill and Melinda Gates Foundation. The gift was the largest donation in the history of charitable giving. The Gates Foundation seeks to further education and fight disease, especially HIV/AIDS, malaria, and tuberculosis throughout the world.

Gasoline prices climbed to a high of almost $4 a gallon in the summer, but by year's end had dropped to below $2 in some areas of the country.

Shootings at rural schools recalled the grim legacy of Columbine High School. On September 29, a 15-year-old in Wisconsin shot and killed his school's principal. A week later, a man invaded an Amish school in rural Pennsylvania and systematically murdered five young girls. In another case, a drifter assaulted his female hostages before killing one of them and himself.

Fans mourned the death of television's Crocodile Hunter Steve Irwin who was killed by a poisonous barb from a stingray while filming a documentary. Irwin, an exuberant and popular naturalist, managed to pull the barb from his chest but died almost immediately after.

DICK LOCHER
Courtesy Chicago Tribune

SCHOOL CHILDREN LEAVING THEIR MARK ON AMERICA

JAMES McCLOSKEY
Courtesy The News-Leader (Va.)

DON LANDGREN, JR.
Courtesy The Landmark (Mass.)

TIM BENSON
Courtesy Argus-Leader (S.D.)

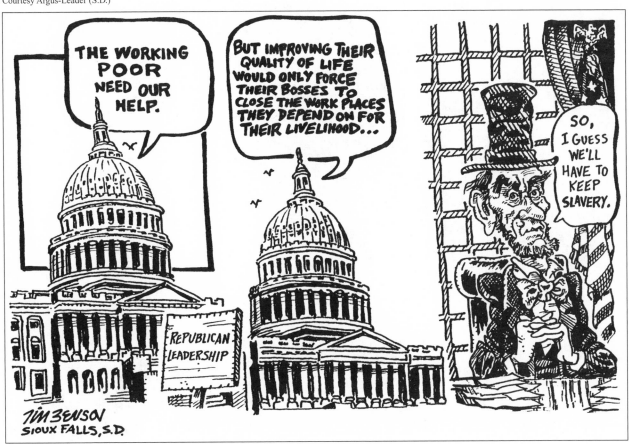

JIM BORGMAN
Courtesy Cincinnati Enquirer

SOMETIME, PERHAPS, IN THE NOT-TOO-DISTANT FUTURE, PEOPLE IN MANY MAIN-LINE DENOMINATION CHURCHES WILL HEAR...

...GOOD NEWS! THE DIVISIVE ISSUE OF THE ORDINATION OF GAYS HAS FINALLY BEEN RESOLVED ONCE AND FOR ALL!

THANK YOU FOR YOUR PATIENCE!

CLAP! CLAP!

CLAP! CLAP!

CLAP! CLAP!

CLAP! CLAP!

CHUCK ASAY
Courtesy Colorado Springs
  Gazette-Telegraph

"YES, EVERYONE SHOULD BE MORE GIVING LIKE WARREN BUFFET...AND NO, I'M NOT INCREASING YOUR ALLOWANCE."

MIKE LESTER
Courtesy Rome News-Tribune (Ga.)

DANIEL FENECH
Courtesy Saline Reporter (Mich.)

ANYBODY WATCH "SURVIVOR" LAST NIGHT? I HEARD THEY DIVIDED THE TEAMS BY RACE...

ANYBODY WATCH "SURVIVOR" LAST NIGHT? I HEARD THEY DIVIDED THE TEAMS BY RACE...

BREAK ROOM

ELENA STEIER
Courtesy The Valley News

STEVE KELLEY
Courtesy The Times-Picayune (La.)

TIM JACKSON
Courtesy Chicago Defender

DAVE SATTLER
Courtesy LaFayette Journal and Courier (Ind.)

JEFF PARKER
Courtesy Florida Today

141

ELIZABETH BRICQUET
Courtesy Kingsport Times-News (Tenn.)

ED FISCHER
Courtesy Rochester Post-Bulletin

CHARLES DANIEL
Courtesy Knoxville News-Sentinel

J. R. ROSE
Courtesy Byrd Newspapers/Daily News Record

BILL GARNER
Courtesy Washington Times

JAMES McCLOSKEY
Courtesy The News-Leader (Va.)

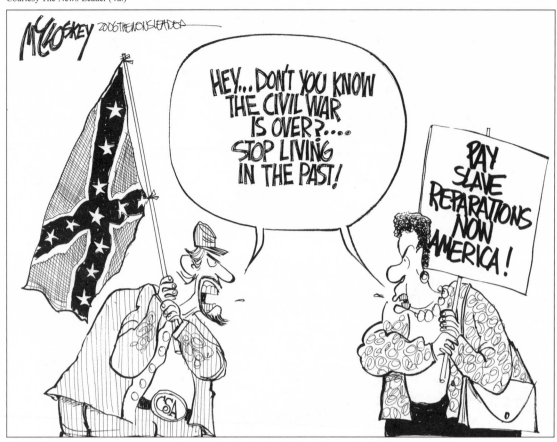

JOHN SHERFFIUS
Courtesy Boulder Daily Camera

RICK KOLLINGER
Courtesy The Star Democrat (Md.)

STEVE BREEN
Courtesy San Diego Union-Tribune

DARREL AKERS
Courtesy The Reporter (Calif.)

SCHOOL DAZE

JIM LANGE
Courtesy Daily Oklahoman

BILL GARNER
Courtesy Washington Times

JIM DYKE
Courtesy Jefferson City News-Tribune

JIM BORGMAN
Courtesy Cincinnati Enquirer

MICHAEL RAMIREZ
Courtesy Investor's Business Daily

147

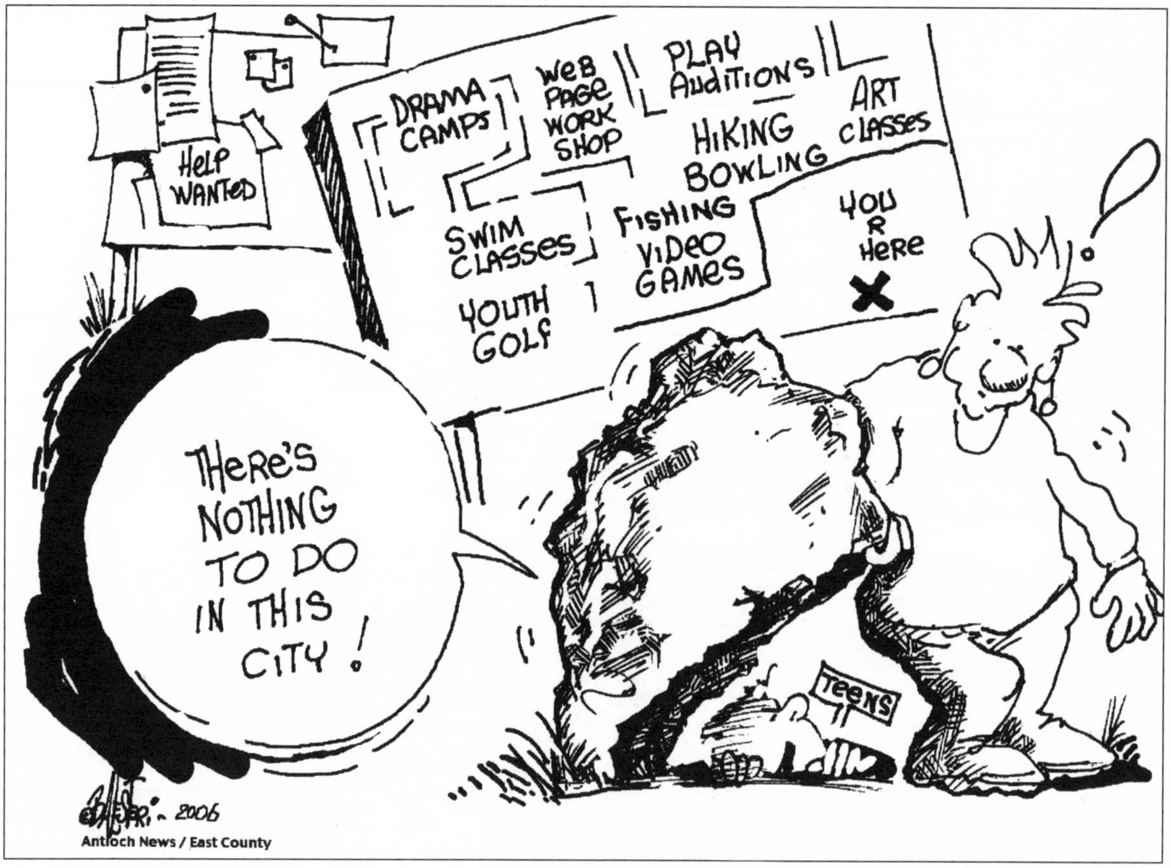
HELP WANTED
DRAMA CAMPS
WEB PAGE WORK SHOP
PLAY AUDITIONS
ART CLASSES
HIKING
BOWLING
SWIM CLASSES
FISHING
VIDEO GAMES
YOU R HERE
YOUTH GOLF
THERE'S NOTHING TO DO IN THIS CITY!
TEENS
2006
Antioch News / East County

ANNETTE BALESTERI
Courtesy Antioch News (Calif.)

STEVE McBRIDE
Courtesy Independence Daily Reporter (Kan.)

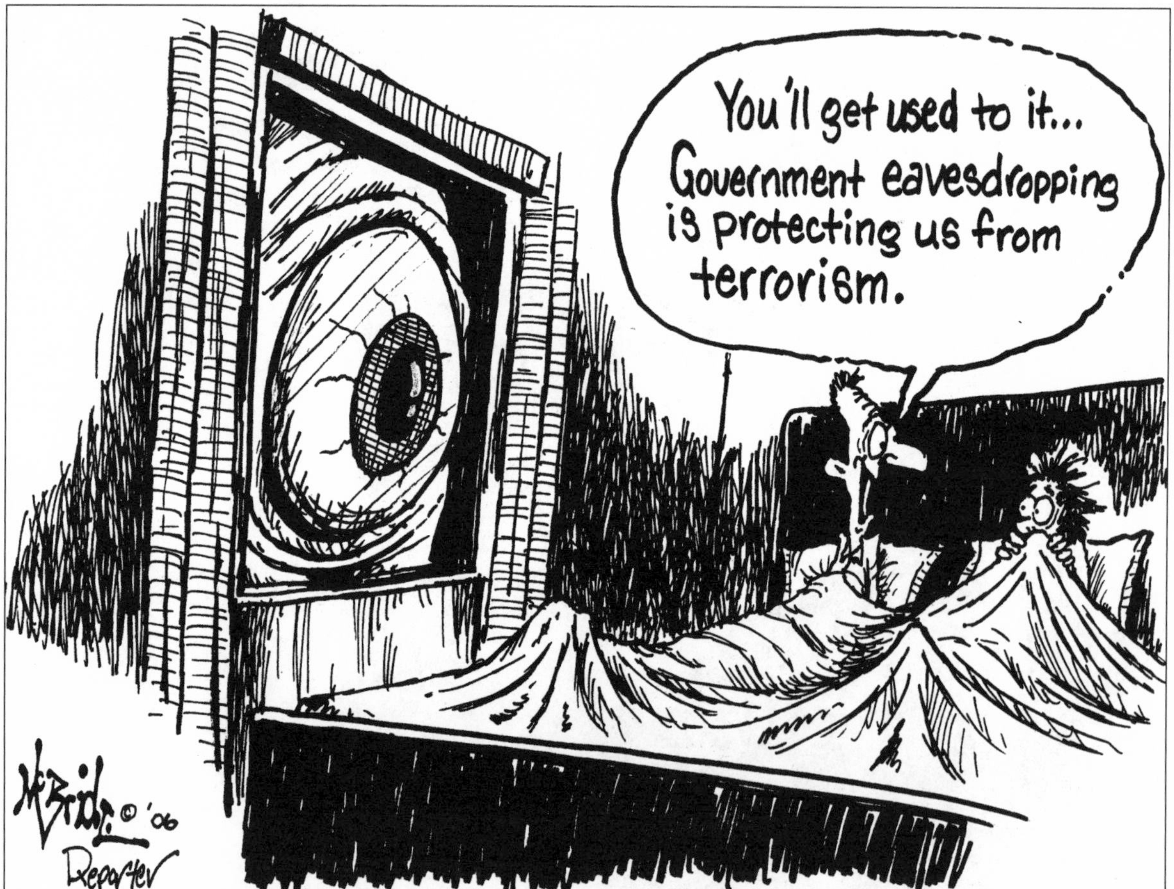
You'll get used to it...
Government eavesdropping is protecting us from terrorism.
McBride © '06
Reporter

Space / Air Travel

The shuttle Discovery docked at the international space station, bringing crewmembers to fully staff the orbiting outpost for the first time since 2003. The Atlantis carried out a 12-day mission and performed construction on the space lab, which is scheduled to be completed in 2010. Fourteen more missions are planned within the next four years.

Airlines have struggled to regain profitability since the terrorist attacks of 9/11. Mergers, cutbacks, and bankruptcies rose during the year as the cost of fuel skyrocketed. In London, a tip that terrorists were planning to use liquid explosives to bring down airliners caused a scare around the world. For a time, some items that travelers normally carry aboard—gels, lotions, and creams—were prohibited. Restrictions on liquids were eased after a time, but tighter security measures remained in effect at airports nationwide.

Tiny Pluto, admired by some as a cosmic underdog but scorned by others who consider it too small and distant, was stripped of its status as a planet by the International Astronomical Union.

STEVE LINDSTROM
Courtesy Duluth News-Tribune

ALAN J. NASH
Courtesy Gering Courier/North Platte Bulletin

JIM LANGE
Courtesy Daily Oklahoman

DON LANDGREN, JR.
Courtesy The Landmark (Mass.)

JIMMY MARGULIES
Courtesy The Record (N.J.)

JAMES D. CROWE
Courtesy Mobile Register

ANN WHITNEY CLEAVES
Courtesy The Palisadian Post (Calif.)

BILL WHITEHEAD
Courtesy Kansas City Business Journal

PETER K. EVANS
Courtesy Islander News (Fla.)

FRANK PAGE
Courtesy Rome Daily Sentinel (N.Y.)

RICHARD B. CROWSON
Courtesy Wichita Eagle

MIKE PETERS
Courtesy Dayton Daily News

grimmy.com

The Media

The New York Times came under fire again for exposing a government program to intercept and block funding for terrorists. The newspaper also disclosed that the super-secret National Security Agency had been conducting warrantless surveillance since 2002 of people in the U.S. with suspected al-Qaida ties.

The power of editorial cartoons was demonstrated during the year. A Danish cartoon depicting the prophet Mohammed wearing a turban shaped like a bomb outraged Muslims and sparked widespread violence. The newspaper that published the cartoon later apologized in an effort to quell the backlash. Military leaders denounced a *Washington Post* cartoon showing Defense Secretary Donald Rumsfeld with an armless, legless soldier.

The made-for-TV movie *Flight 93* was released. It depicted the heroism of passengers aboard the hijacked plane that crashed into a Pennsylvania field on 9/11. The best-selling book of the year was *The Da Vinci Code,* a controversial tale based on the idea that Jesus fathered a child with Mary Magdalene. It sold 40 million copies.

Actor Mel Gibson made anti-Semitic comments that stained his public image after being arrested for drunk driving.

REX BABIN
Courtesy Sacramento Bee

JIM BUSH
Courtesy Providence Journal (R.I.)

JAKE FULLER
Courtesy Gainesville Sun

JOE HELLER
Courtesy Green Bay Press-Gazette

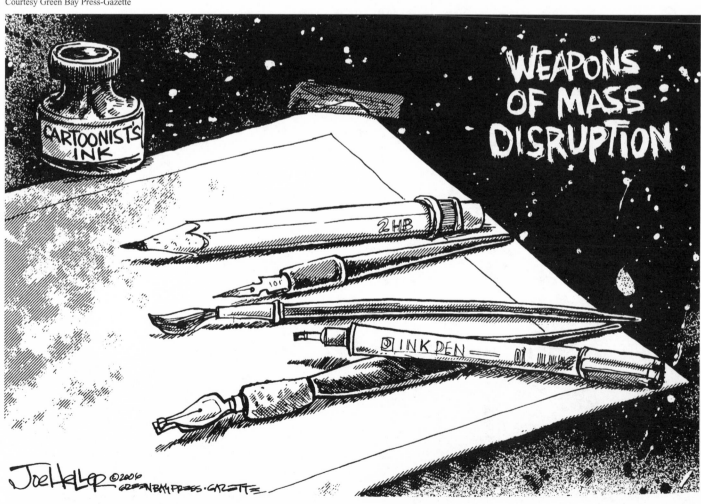

THE SELF-FULFILLING PROPHET...

MIKE LESTER
Courtesy Rome News-Tribune (Ga.)

BOB ENGLEHART
Courtesy Hartford Courant

CLAY JONES
Courtesy Free Lance-Star (Va.)

MIKE LESTER
Courtesy Rome News-Tribune (Ga.)

CHARLES DANIEL
Courtesy Knoxville News-Sentinel

WILL TAKE MORE THAN A GRAIN!

JACK JURDEN
Courtesy Wilmington News Journal

JUSTIN DeFREITAS
Courtesy Berkeley Daily Planet

MR. CHENEY, DID YOU SHOOT THAT GUY?   WAS IT YOUR FIRST?   HOW DID IT FEEL?

MR. LANDIS, ARE YOU A JUICER?   SAY IT AIN'T SO, FLOYD!   DIDJA DO IT? HUH? DIDJA? DIDJA?

MR. KARR, ARE YOU A KILLER?   SAY IT'S SO, JOHN!   DIDJA DO IT? HUH? DIDJA? DIDJA?

HURRICANE KATRINA: ONE YEAR LATER   OH, THE HUMANITY!   ANY OF YOU BLACK FOLK CARE TO GO ON CAMERA?

WHY DO WE KEEP RUNNING BACK AND FORTH?   BALANCE.

159

ALAN VITELLO
Courtesy Greeley Tribune

STEVE BREEN
Courtesy San Diego Union-Tribune

ED GAMBLE
Courtesy Florida Times-Union

CLAY JONES
Courtesy Free Lance-Star (Va.)

GARY VARVEL
Courtesy Indianapolis Star

BRUCE BEATTIE
Courtesy Daytona Beach News-Journal

WALT HANDELSMAN
Courtesy Newsday

CHUCK LEGGE
Courtesy The Frontiersman

TOM STIGLICH
Courtesy Northeast Times (Pa.)

PAUL FELL
Courtesy Lincoln Journal Star

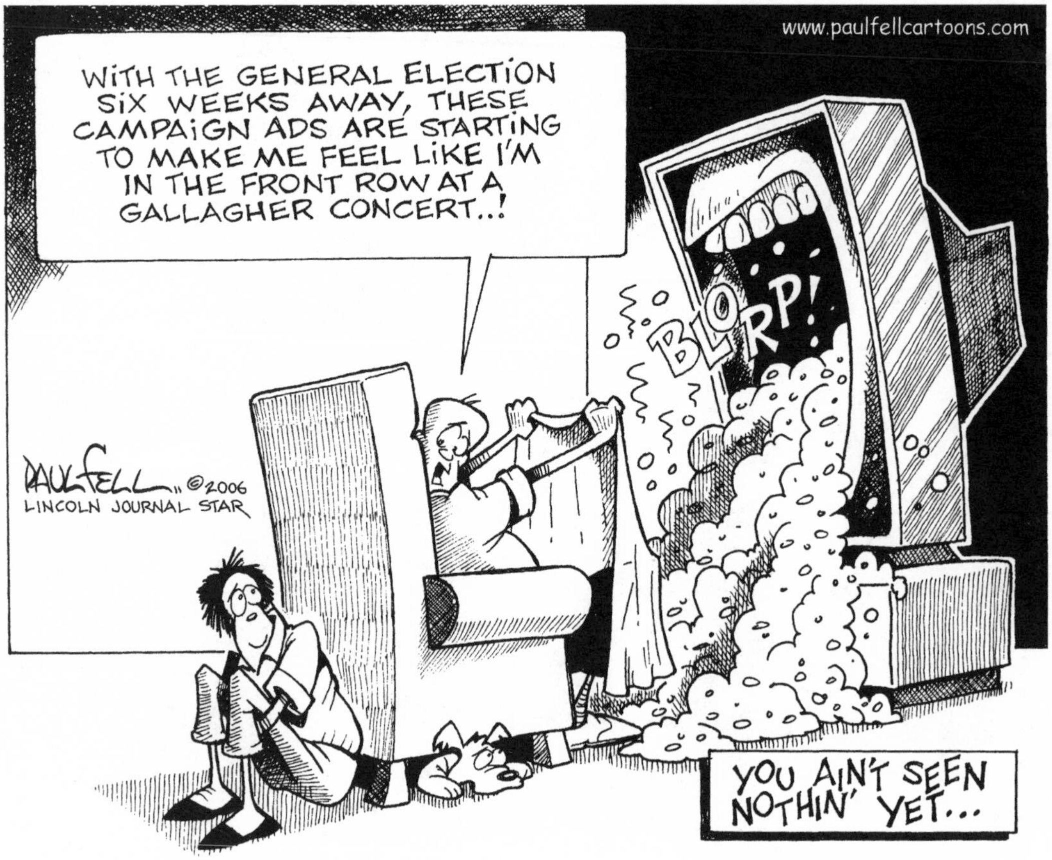

www.paulfellcartoons.com
WITH THE GENERAL ELECTION SIX WEEKS AWAY, THESE CAMPAIGN ADS ARE STARTING TO MAKE ME FEEL LIKE I'M IN THE FRONT ROW AT A GALLAGHER CONCERT..!
BLORP!
PAUL FELL ©2006 LINCOLN JOURNAL STAR
YOU AIN'T SEEN NOTHIN' YET...

AARON TAYLOR
Courtesy The Daily Herald (Utah)

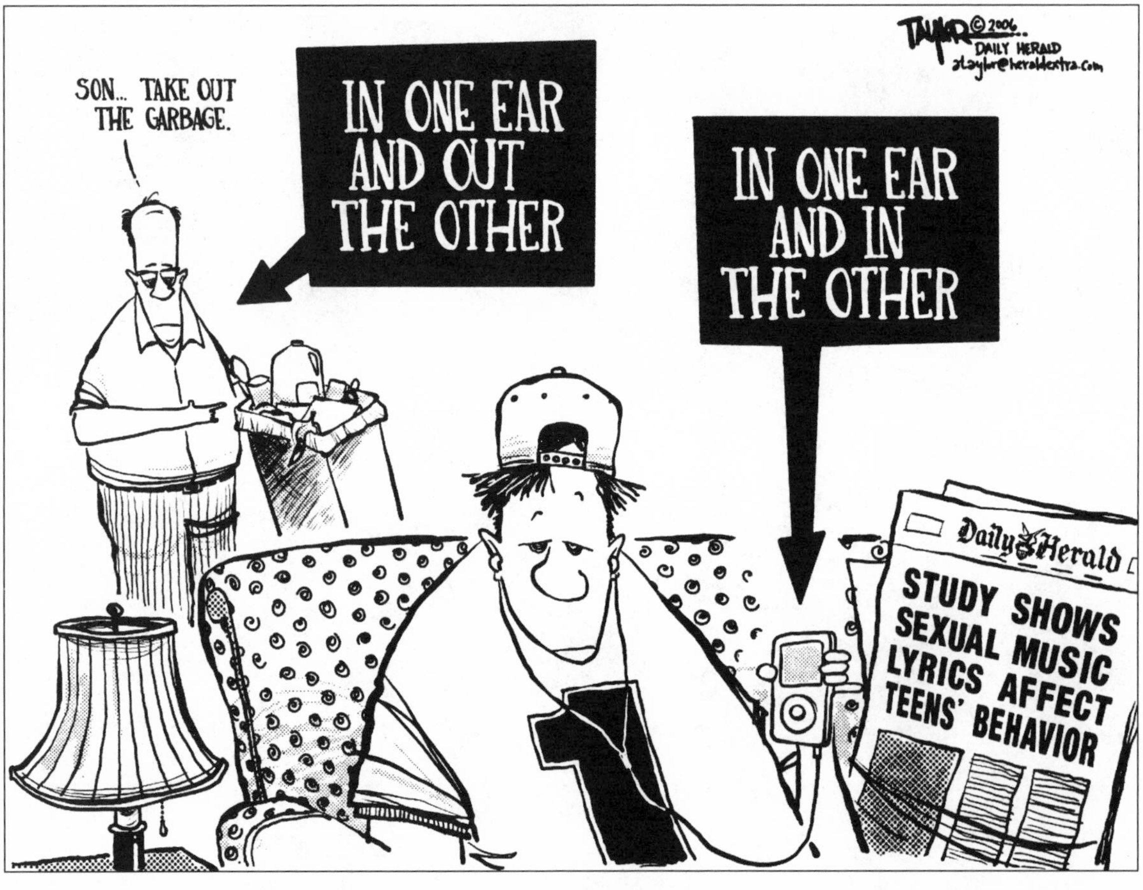

TAYLOR ©2006 DAILY HERALD ataylor@heraldextra.com
SON... TAKE OUT THE GARBAGE.
IN ONE EAR AND OUT THE OTHER
IN ONE EAR AND IN THE OTHER
Daily Herald
STUDY SHOWS SEXUAL MUSIC LYRICS AFFECT TEENS' BEHAVIOR

DAVID DONAR
Courtesy Macomb Daily (Miss.)

JACK HIGGINS
Courtesy Chicago Sun-Times

BILL GARNER
Courtesy Washington Times

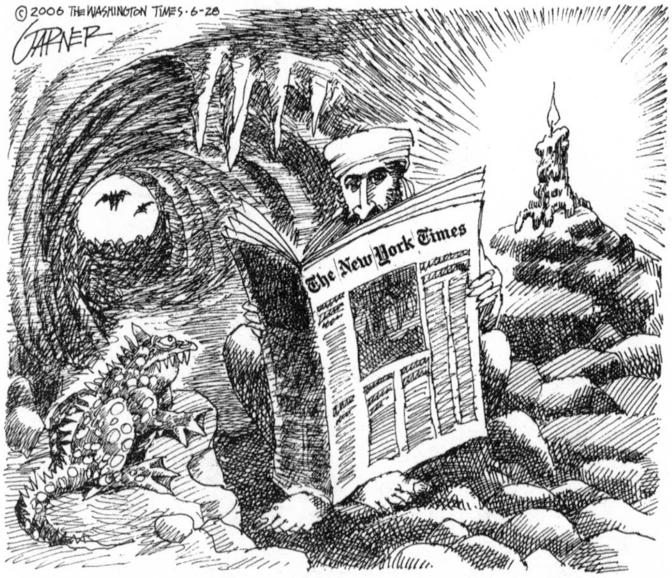
©2006 THE WASHINGTON TIMES·6-28
GARNER
The New York Times

FRANK PAGE
Courtesy Rome Daily Sentinel (N.Y.)

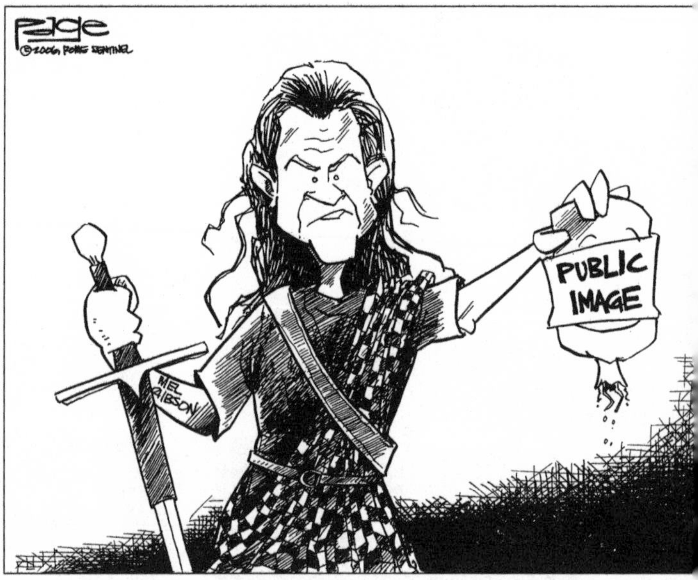
PAGE
©2006 ROME SENTINEL
MEL GIBSON
PUBLIC IMAGE

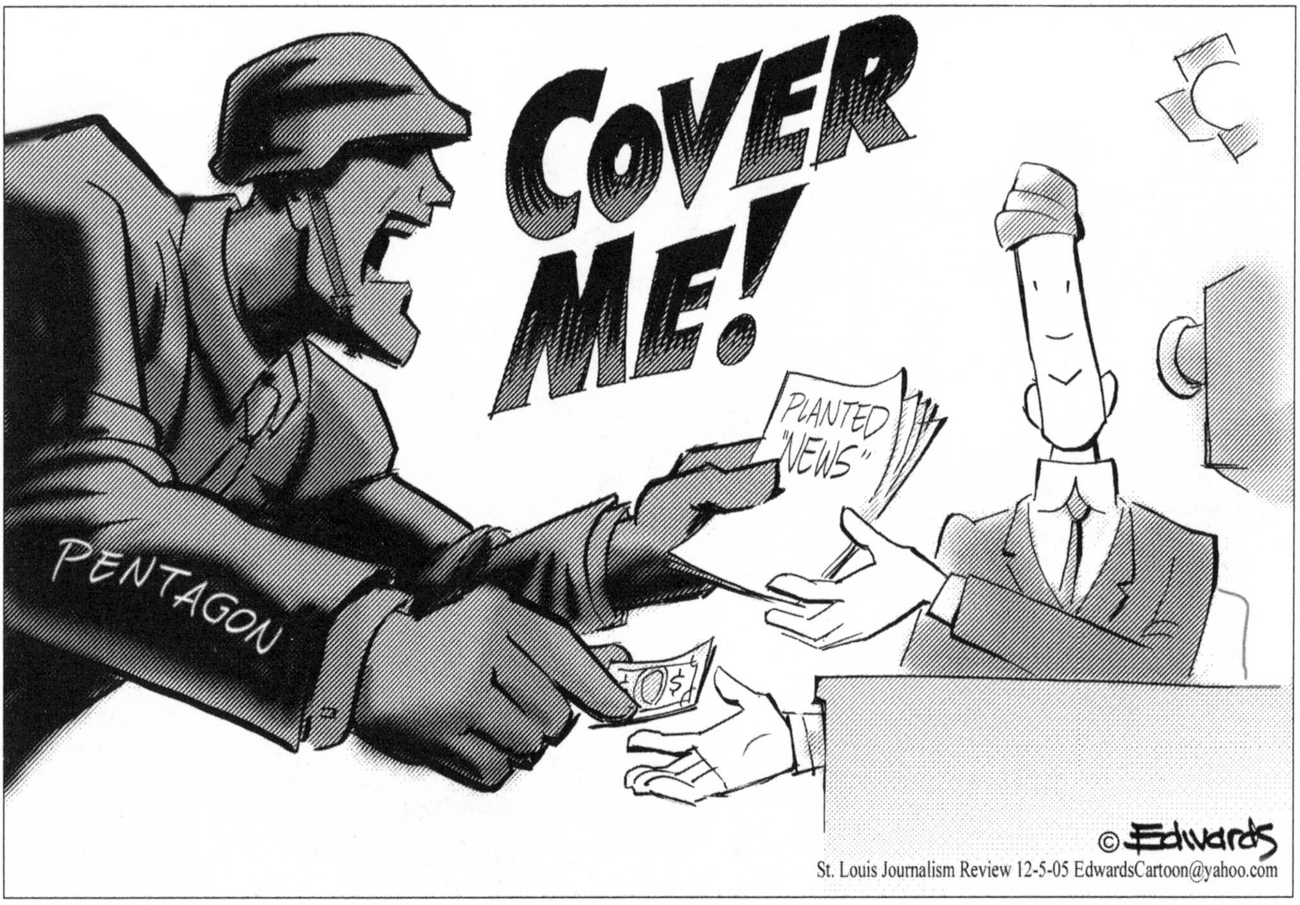
COVER ME!
PLANTED "NEWS"
PENTAGON
© Edwards
St. Louis Journalism Review 12-5-05 EdwardsCartoon@yahoo.com

STEVE EDWARDS
Courtesy St. Louis Journalism Review

MICHAEL RAMIREZ
Courtesy Investor's Business Daily

ROB ROGERS
Courtesy Pittsburgh Post-Gazette

JOEL PETT
Courtesy Lexington Herald-Leader

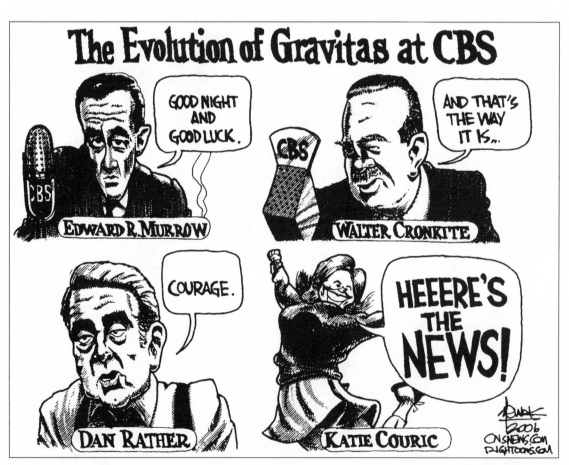

PAUL NOWAK
Courtesy Scripps-Howard Service

RANDY BISH
Courtesy Tribune-Review (Pa.)

SCOTT STANTIS
Courtesy Birmingham News

DON LANDGREN, JR.
Courtesy The Landmark (Mass.)

JERRY HOLBERT
Courtesy Boston Herald

STEVE McBRIDE
Courtesy Independence Daily Reporter (Kan.)

BRUCE QUAST
Courtesy Rockford Register-Star (Ill.)

JEFF STAHLER
Courtesy Columbus Dispatch

NEIL GRAHAME
Courtesy Spencer Newspapers

JOHN RILEY
Courtesy Johnrileycartoons.com

The Economy

The price of oil soared to a record $74 a barrel, and motorists screamed as gas prices at the pump approached $4 a gallon. As gasoline prices rose, interest in the production of coal increased, despite environmental concerns. By year's end, however, the price of a gallon of gasoline had dropped to below $2 in some markets.

This good news eased inflation pressures, boosted the stock market, and buoyed consumer confidence. Average weekly earnings for workers in the private sector showed a small increase, an improvement over the previous year when wages fell. At the same time, the unemployment rate dropped to 4.7 percent.

Before the end of 2006 the economy had recorded improvement in 23 consecutive quarters. The stock market set new records, with the Dow Jones Industrial Average passing the historic 12,000 mark. The business boom helped reduce the federal deficit to a four-year low.

Things have not gone well, however, for all U.S. companies. General Motors and Ford were forced to close some plants and lay off hundreds of workers because of stiff competition from abroad. Toyota is expected to overtake General Motors as the world's largest carmaker before the end of 2007.

STEVE BREEN
Courtesy San Diego Union-Tribune

JOE MAJESKI
Courtesy The Times-Leader (Pa.)

GRAEME MacKAY
Courtesy Hamilton Spectator (Canada)

JEFF DANZIGER
Courtesy NYTS/CWS

174

PEDRO MOLINA
Courtesy El Nuevo Diario

ROB ROGERS
Courtesy Pittsburgh Post-Gazette

ERIC SMITH
Courtesy Annapolis Capital-Gazette

JIM LANGE
Courtesy Daily Oklahoman

LARRY WRIGHT
Courtesy Detroit News

176

MARTY RISKIN
Courtesy Melrose Free Press (Mass.)

MARTY STEIN
Courtesy La Prensa (Fla.)

JON RICHARDS
Courtesy Albuquerque Journal North

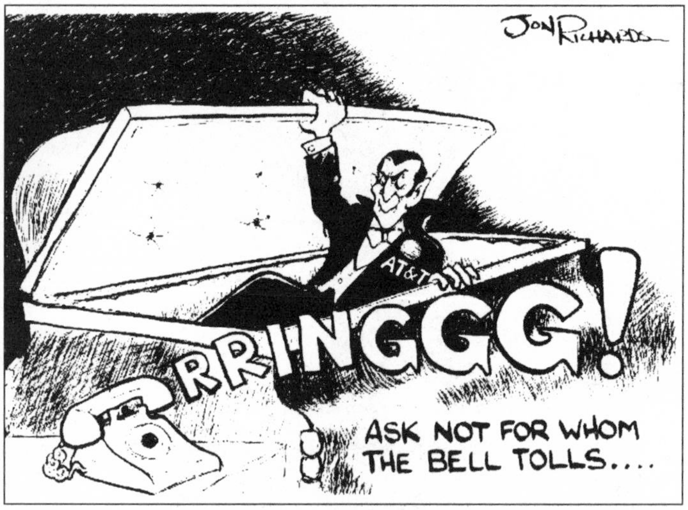
JON RICHARDS
AT&T
RRINGGG!
ASK NOT FOR WHOM THE BELL TOLLS....

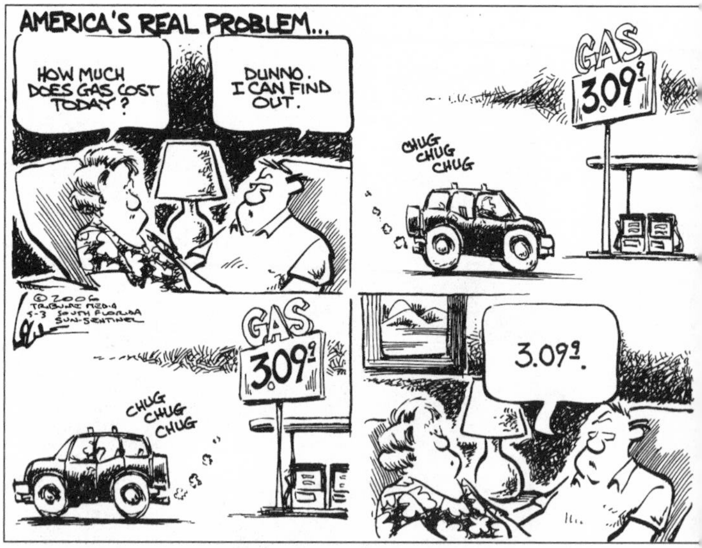
AMERICA'S REAL PROBLEM...
HOW MUCH DOES GAS COST TODAY?
DUNNO. I CAN FIND OUT.
GAS 3.09⁹
CHUG CHUG CHUG
GAS 3.09⁹
CHUG CHUG CHUG
3.09⁹.

CHAN LOWE
Courtesy Fort Lauderdale News/Sun Sentinel

JEFF PARKER
Courtesy Florida Today

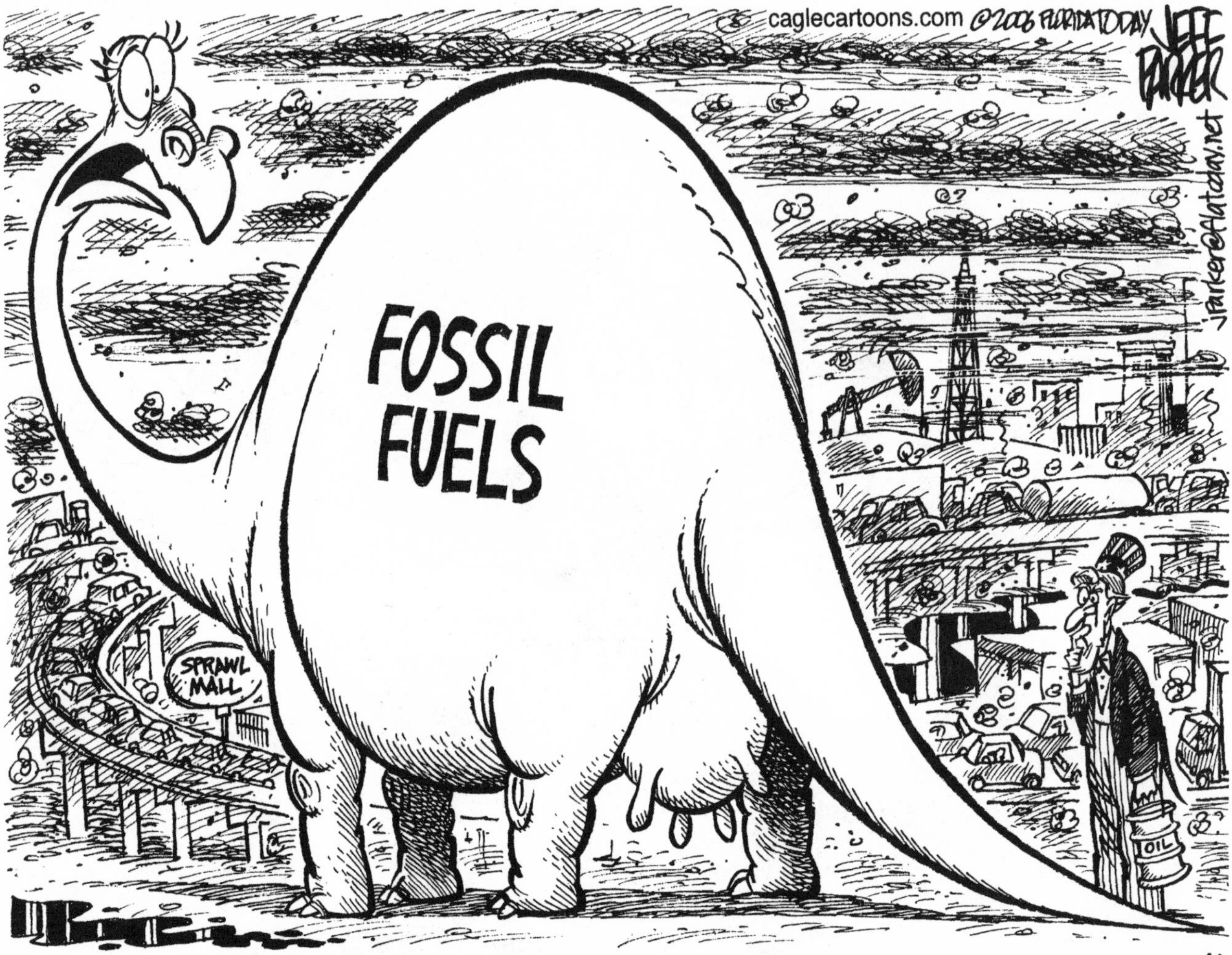
caglecartoons.com ©2006 FLORIDA TODAY JEFF PARKER
jparker@flatoday.net
FOSSIL FUELS
SPRAWL MALL
OIL
"JUST LIKE THAT? YOU'RE GOING TO WEAN YOURSELF OFF OIL? AND AFTER ALL I'VE DONE FOR YOU!"

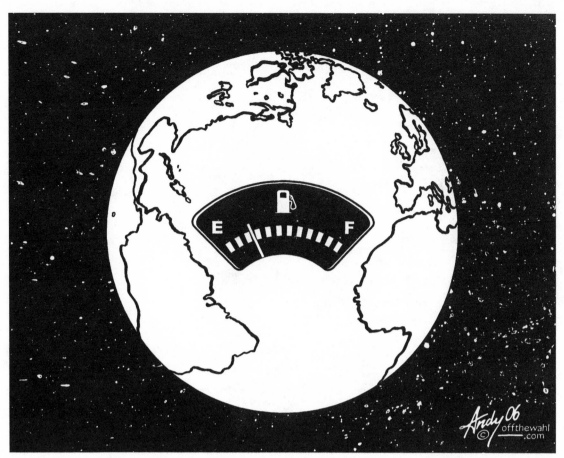

ANDREW WAHL
Courtesy Wenatchee World (Wash.)

ROSS GOSSE
Courtesy Pine Tree Syndicate

ED COLLEY
Courtesy Boston Globe South

DAVE SATTLER
Courtesy LaFayette Journal and Courier (Ind.)

BRUCE BEATTIE
Courtesy Daytona Beach News-Journal

180

JOHN AUCHTER
Courtesy Grand Rapids Business Journal

JOSEPH RANK
Courtesy Times-Press Recorder (Calif.)

MIKE KEEFE
Courtesy Denver Post

"Forget ethanol, hydrogen, helium, or steam. What WE need is a car that can run on the carcasses of greedy oil executives!"

Canada

Conservatives swept into power early in the year, pushing aside the scandal-plagued Liberal Party that had ruled Canada for thirteen years. The Liberals experienced severely strained relations with the U.S., condemning the war in Iraq, refusing to join the continental anti-ballistic missile plan, and criticizing President Bush for rejecting the Kyoto Protocol on greenhouse gas emissions.

Canada and the United States announced an agreement to settle a decades-long trade battle over softwood lumber, a major home-building component. Canada's $10 billion in annual shipments of softwood lumber to the U.S. represents about one-third of America's market. Under the agreement, Canada's share of the U.S. market would not exceed 34 percent. To protect U.S. producers, Canada will impose an export tax of up to 15 percent, depending on the market price.

An alleged home-grown ring of terrorists was uncovered in June. Seventeen Muslim men were charged with conducting terrorist training and plotting to build bombs. Their alleged targets included Toronto's landmark CN Tower and the Peace Tower of the Parliament building in Ottawa.

CHRIS BRITT
Courtesy State Journal-Register (Ill.)

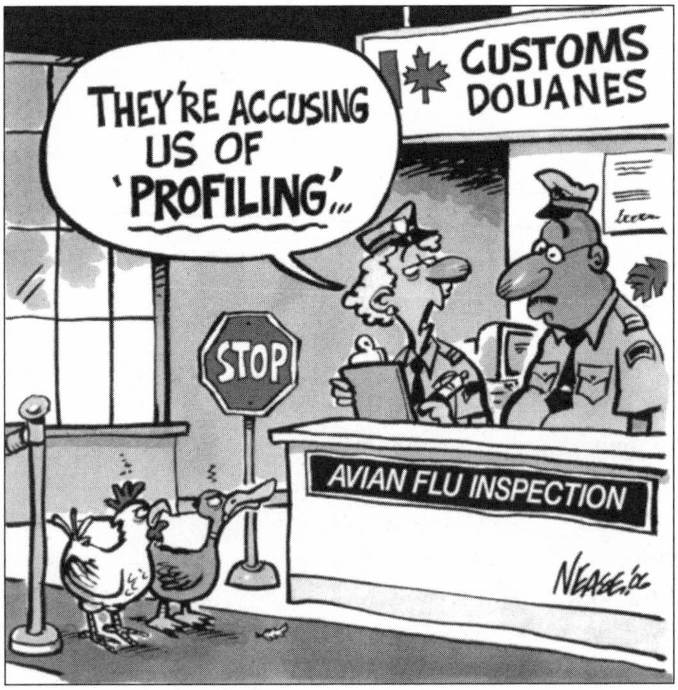
THEY'RE ACCUSING US OF 'PROFILING'...
CUSTOMS
DOUANES
STOP
AVIAN FLU INSPECTION
NEASE '06

STEVE NEASE
Courtesy Toronto Sun

STEVE NEASE
Courtesy Vancouver Sun

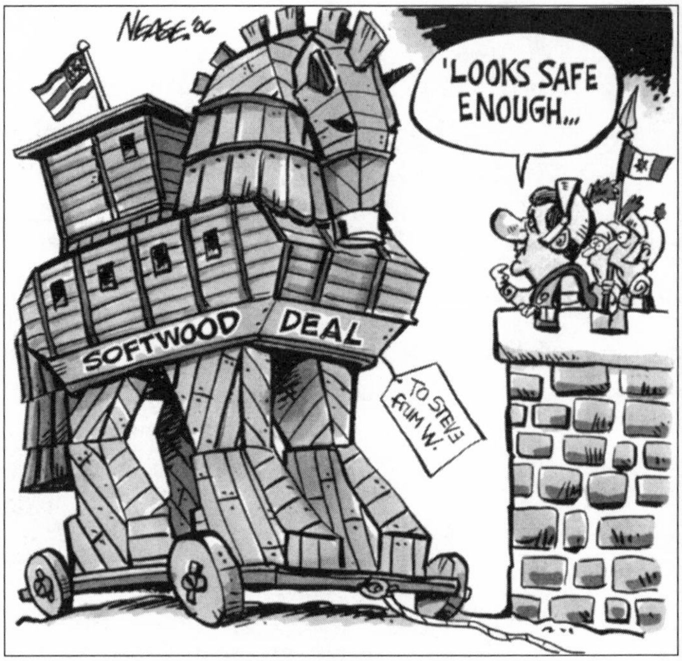
NEASE '06
'LOOKS SAFE ENOUGH...
SOFTWOOD
DEAL
TO STEVE FRUM W.

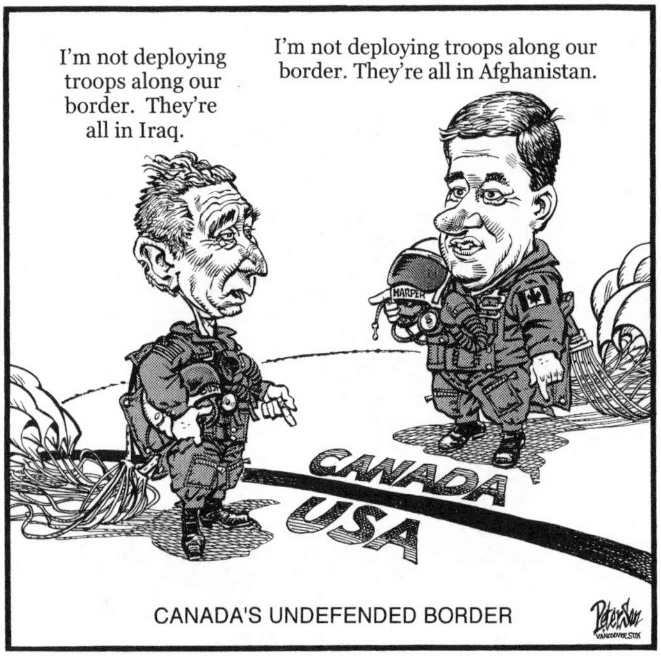
I'm not deploying troops along our border. They're all in Iraq.
I'm not deploying troops along our border. They're all in Afghanistan.
HARPER
CANADA
USA
Peterson

CANADA'S UNDEFENDED BORDER

ROY PETERSON
Courtesy Vancouver Sun

ROY PETERSON
Courtesy Vancouver Sun

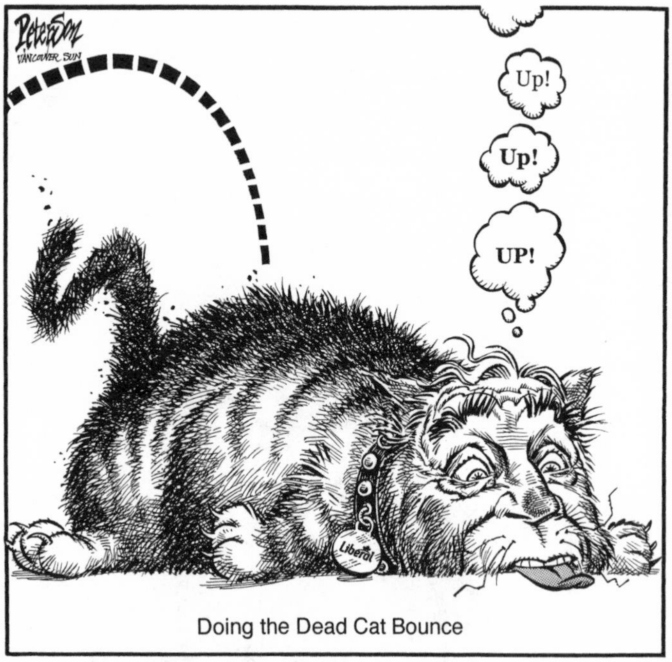
Peterson
Vancouver Sun
Up!
Up!
UP!
Liberal

Doing the Dead Cat Bounce

BOB LANG
Courtesy The Pilot News (Ind.)

GRAEME MacKAY
Courtesy Hamilton Spectator (Canada)

STEVE NEASE
Courtesy Toronto Sun

JEFF DANZIGER
Courtesy NYTS/CWS

STEVE NEASE
Courtesy Brantford Expositor (Canada)

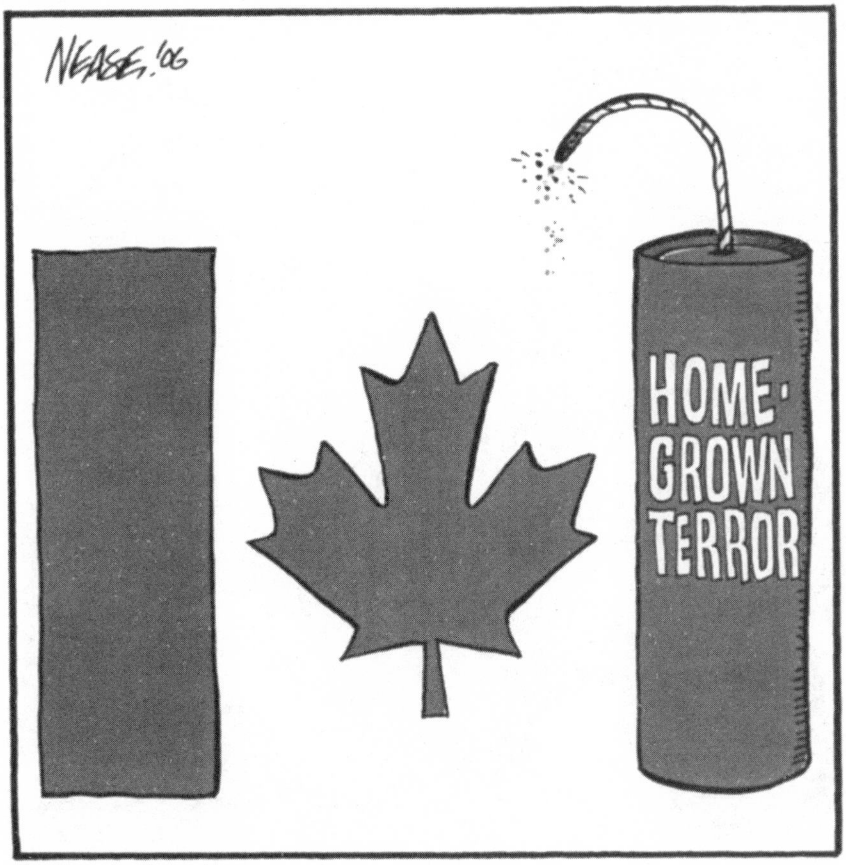
NEASE.'06
HOME-GROWN TERROR

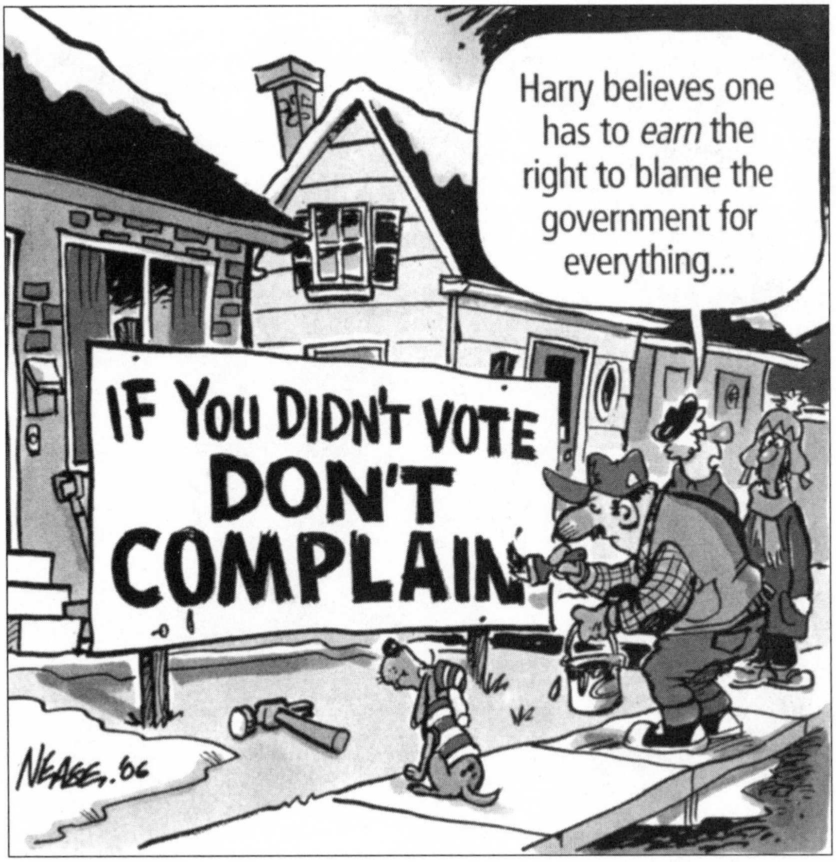
Harry believes one has to *earn* the right to blame the government for everything...
IF YOU DIDN'T VOTE DON'T COMPLAIN
NEASE.'06

STEVE NEASE
Courtesy Hamilton Spectator (Canada)

RICK KOLLINGER
Courtesy The Star Democrat (Md.)

JERRY HOLBERT
Courtesy Boston Herald

... and Other Issues

In an address in his home country, Pope Benedict XVI quoted a statement by a Byzantine emperor disparaging Islam. He did not say that he agreed with the quotation, but declared that religious conversions should not be sought by force. Many Muslims took offense, rioted in a number of cities, and demanded an apology. The pope apologized.

The United Nations continued as an ineffectual organization, internally corrupt and unwilling to halt the slaughter in Darfur or intervene seriously in the Israeli-Hezbollah conflict in Lebanon. U.N. members applauded remarks by Venezuelan despot Hugo Chavez referring to President Bush as "the devil."

The Senate confirmed Samuel Alito's appointment to the Supreme Court despite efforts by Democrats to stop it, and FBI agents searched a Michigan farm for the body of long-missing Jimmy Hoffa. They found nothing. An explosion in a West Virginia coal mine killed 14 miners. It appeared that their emergency oxygen supplies might have failed.

Former President Jimmy Carter was widely castigated for using the funeral of Coretta Scott King, widow of Martin Luther King, Jr., to criticize Bush Administration policies. Other notables who died during the year included Don Knotts, Steve Irwin, Dennis Weaver, Glenn Ford, and Darren McGavin.

BOB LANG
Courtesy The Pilot News (Ind.)

DOING WHAT THEY DO BEST

JOE MAJESKI
Courtesy The Times-Leader (Pa.)

RANDY BISH
Courtesy Tribune-Review (Pa.)

SUNSHINE AND THE PRETTIEST CLOUDS YOU'VE EVER SEEN...
LOOKS LIKE WE'RE STILL IN WEST VIRGINIA, FELLAS

The True Cost of Electricity

JEFF DANZIGER
Courtesy NYTS/CWS

ED GAMBLE
Courtesy Florida Times-Union

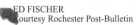
ED FISCHER
Courtesy Rochester Post-Bulletin

J. R. ROSE
Courtesy Byrd Newspapers/Daily News Record

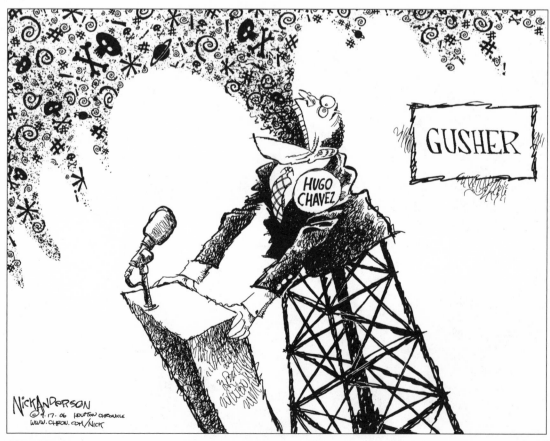

NICK ANDERSON
Courtesy Houston Chronicle

PAUL COMBS
Courtesy Tampa Tribune

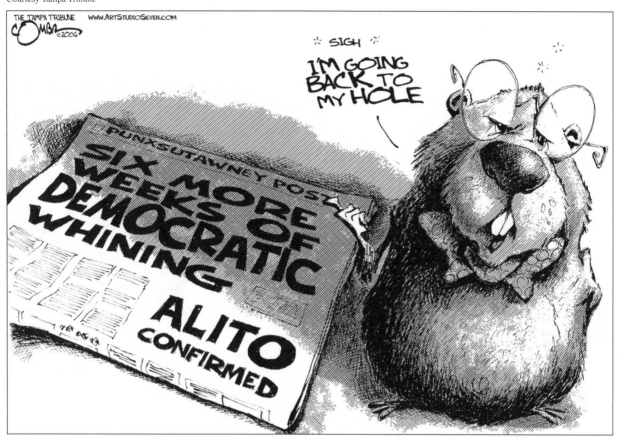

GARY MARKSTEIN
Courtesy Copley News Service

PAUL CONRAD
Courtesy Tribune Media Services

FRANK PAGE
Courtesy Rome Daily Sentinel (N.Y

JACK HIGGINS
Courtesy Chicago Sun-Times

DENNIS DRAUGHON
Courtesy Fayetteville Observer

STEVE SACK
Courtesy Minneapolis Star-Tribune

195

J. R. ROSE
Courtesy Byrd Newspapers/Daily News Record

BILL JANOCHA
Courtesy Stamford Times

STEVE KELLEY
Courtesy The Times-Picayune (La.)

MARK STREETER
Courtesy Savannah Morning News

GARY VARVEL
Courtesy Indianapolis Star

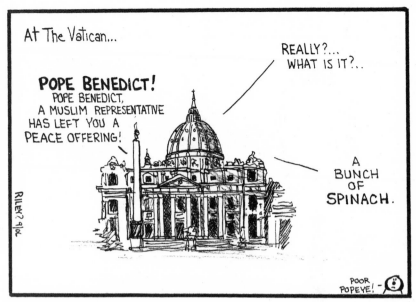

JOHN RILEY
Courtesy Johnrileycartoons.com

STEVE BREEN
Courtesy San Diego Union-Tribune

STEVE LINDSTROM
Courtesy Duluth News-Tribune

RANDY BISH
Courtesy Tribune-Review (Pa.)

NEIL GRAHAME
Courtesy Spencer Newspapers

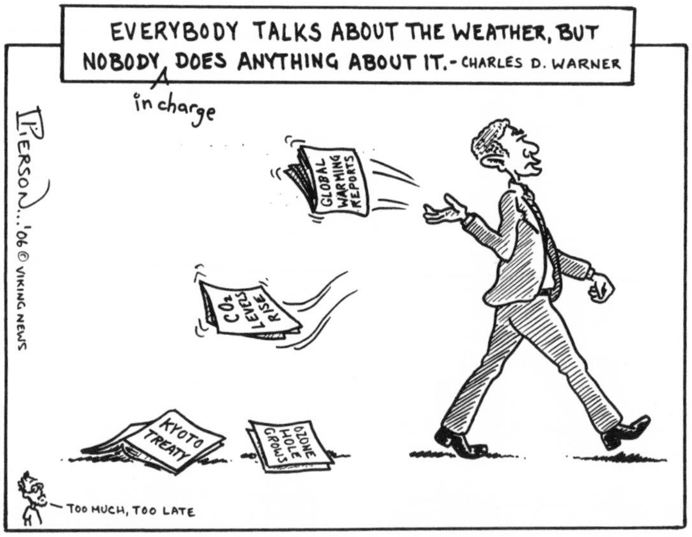
EVERYBODY TALKS ABOUT THE WEATHER, BUT NOBODY in charge DOES ANYTHING ABOUT IT. - CHARLES D. WARNER
GLOBAL WARMING REPORTS
CO2 LEVELS RISE
KYOTO TREATY
OZONE HOLE GROWS
TOO MUCH, TOO LATE
PIERSON '06 © VIKING NEWS

SCOTT-ALLEN PIERSON
Courtesy The Viking News

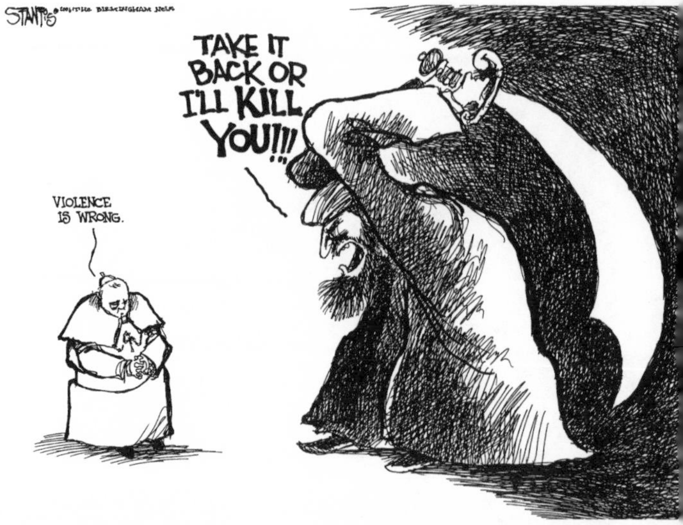
TAKE IT BACK OR I'LL KILL YOU!!!
VIOLENCE IS WRONG.
STANTIS

SCOTT STANTIS
Courtesy Birmingham New

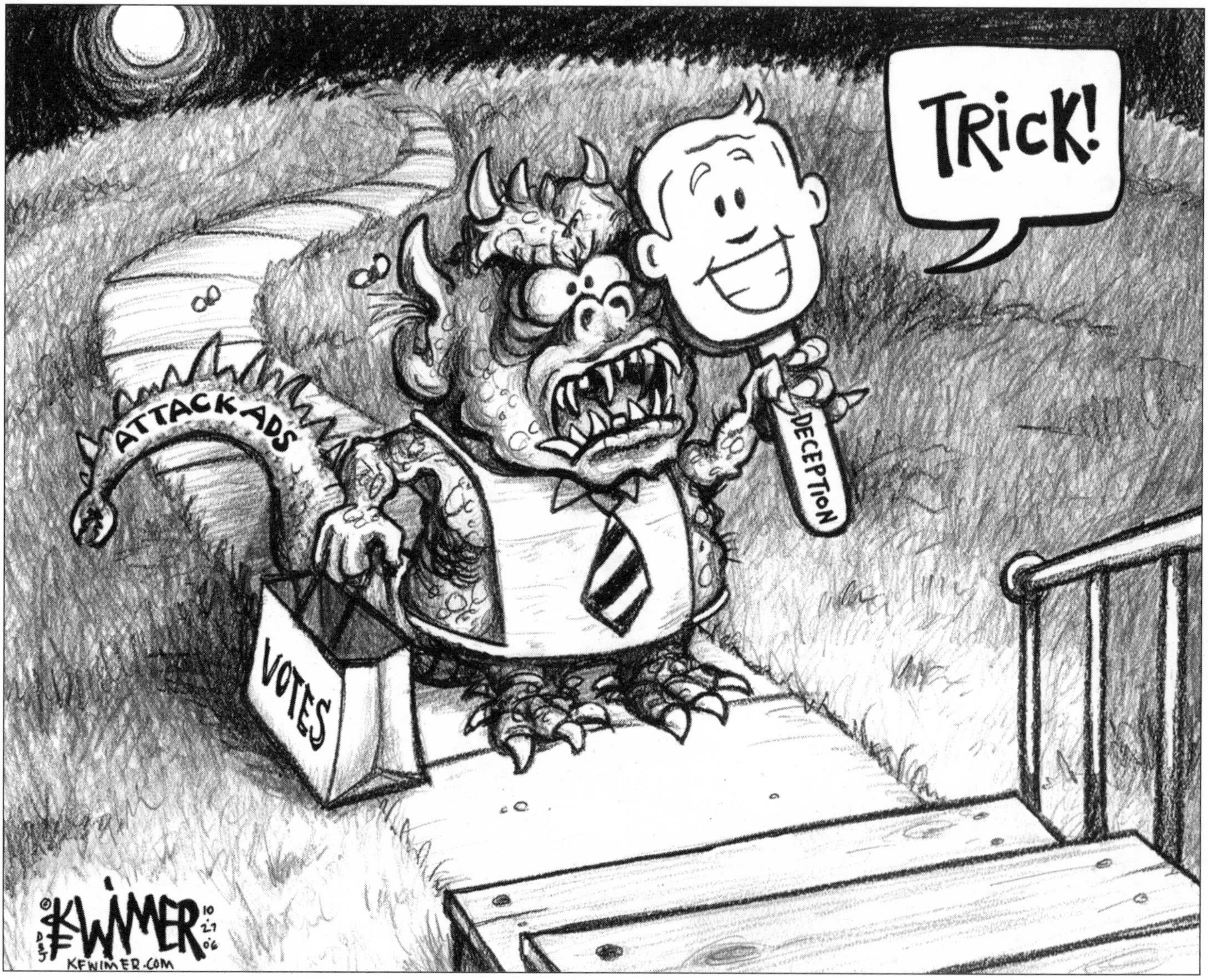
TRICK!
ATTACK ADS
DECEPTION
VOTES
KWIMER 10 27 06
KFWIMER.COM

KARL WIMER
Courtesy Denver Business Journal

PAUL CONRAD
Courtesy Tribune Media Services

DANA SUMMERS
Courtesy Orlando Sentinel

PETER DUNLAP-SHOHL
Courtesy Anchorage Daily News

Which **voting machine** is most vulnerable to partisan hackers?

STEVE EDWARDS
Courtesy St. Louis Journalism Review

Past Award Winners

PULITZER PRIZE

1922—Rollin Kirby, New York World
1923—No award given
1924—J.N. Darling, New York Herald-Tribune
1925—Rollin Kirby, New York World
1926—D.R. Fitzpatrick, St. Louis Post-Dispatch
1927—Nelson Harding, Brooklyn Eagle
1928—Nelson Harding, Brooklyn Eagle
1929—Rollin Kirby, New York World
1930—Charles Macauley, Brooklyn Eagle
1931—Edmund Duffy, Baltimore Sun
1932—John T. McCutcheon, Chicago Tribune
1933—H.M. Talburt, Washington Daily News
1934—Edmund Duffy, Baltimore Sun
1935—Ross A. Lewis, Milwaukee Journal
1936—No award given
1937—C.D. Batchelor, New York Daily News
1938—Vaughn Shoemaker, Chicago Daily News
1939—Charles G. Werner, Daily Oklahoman
1940—Edmund Duffy, Baltimore Sun
1941—Jacob Burck, Chicago Times
1942—Herbert L. Block, NEA
1943—Jay N. Darling, New York Herald-Tribune
1944—Clifford K. Berryman, Washington Star
1945—Bill Mauldin, United Features Syndicate
1946—Bruce Russell, Los Angeles Times
1947—Vaughn Shoemaker, Chicago Daily News
1948—Reuben L. ("Rube") Goldberg, New York Sun
1949—Lute Pease, Newark Evening News
1950—James T. Berryman, Washington Star
1951—Reginald W. Manning, Arizona Republic
1952—Fred L. Packer, New York Mirror
1953—Edward D. Kuekes, Cleveland Plain Dealer
1954—Herbert L. Block, Washington Post
1955—Daniel R. Fitzpatrick, St. Louis Post-Dispatch
1956—Robert York, Louisville Times
1957—Tom Little, Nashville Tennessean
1958—Bruce M. Shanks, Buffalo Evening News
1959—Bill Mauldin, St. Louis Post-Dispatch
1960—No award given
1961—Carey Orr, Chicago Tribune
1962—Edmund S. Valtman, Hartford Times
1963—Frank Miller, Des Moines Register
1964—Paul Conrad, Denver Post
1965—No award given
1966—Don Wright, Miami News
1967—Patrick B. Oliphant, Denver Post
1968—Eugene Gray Payne, Charlotte Observer
1969—John Fischetti, Chicago Daily News
1970—Thomas F. Darcy, Newsday
1971—Paul Conrad, Los Angeles Times
1972—Jeffrey K. MacNelly, Richmond News Leader
1973—No award given
1974—Paul Szep, Boston Globe
1975—Garry Trudeau, Universal Press Syndicate
1976—Tony Auth, Philadelphia Enquirer

1977—Paul Szep, Boston Globe
1978—Jeff MacNelly, Richmond News Leader
1979—Herbert Block, Washington Post
1980—Don Wright, Miami News
1981—Mike Peters, Dayton Daily News
1982—Ben Sargent, Austin American-Statesman
1983—Dick Locher, Chicago Tribune
1984—Paul Conrad, Los Angeles Times
1985—Jeff MacNelly, Chicago Tribune
1986—Jules Feiffer, Universal Press Syndicate
1987—Berke Breathed, Washington Post Writers Group
1988—Doug Marlette, Atlanta Constitution
1989—Jack Higgins, Chicago Sun-Times
1990—Tom Toles, Buffalo News
1991—Jim Borgman, Cincinnati Enquirer
1992—Signe Wilkinson, Philadelphia Daily News
1993—Steve Benson, Arizona Republic
1994—Michael Ramirez, Memphis Commercial Appeal
1995—Mike Luckovich, Atlanta Constitution
1996—Jim Morin, Miami Herald
1997—Walt Handelsman, New Orleans Times-Picayune
1998—Steve Breen, Asbury Park Press
1999—David Horsey, Seattle Post-Intelligencer
2000—Joel Pett, Lexington Herald-Leader
2001—Ann Telnaes, Tribune Media Services
2002—Clay Bennett, Christian Science Monitor
2003—David Horsey, Seattle Post-Intelligencer
2004—Matt Davies, The Journal News
2005—Nick Anderson, Louisville Courier-Journal
2006—Mike Luckovich, Atlanta Journal-Constitution

NATIONAL SOCIETY OF PROFESSIONAL JOURNALISTS AWARD (SIGMA DELTA CHI AWARD)

1942—Jacob Burck, Chicago Times
1943—Charles Werner, Chicago Sun
1944—Henry Barrow, Associated Press
1945—Reuben L. Goldberg, New York Sun
1946—Dorman H. Smith, NEA
1947—Bruce Russell, Los Angeles Times
1948—Herbert Block, Washington Post
1949—Herbert Block, Washington Post
1950—Bruce Russell, Los Angeles Times
1951—Herbert Block, Washington Post and
        Bruce Russell, Los Angeles Times
1952—Cecil Jensen, Chicago Daily News
1953—John Fischetti, NEA
1954—Calvin Alley, Memphis Commercial Appeal
1955—John Fischetti, NEA
1956—Herbert Block, Washington Post
1957—Scott Long, Minneapolis Tribune
1958—Clifford H. Baldowski, Atlanta Constitution
1959—Charles G. Brooks, Birmingham News

PAST AWARD WINNERS

1960—Dan Dowling, New York Herald-Tribune
1961—Frank Interlandi, Des Moines Register
1962—Paul Conrad, Denver Post
1963—William Mauldin, Chicago Sun-Times
1964—Charles Bissell, Nashville Tennessean
1965—Roy Justus, Minneapolis Star
1966—Patrick Oliphant, Denver Post
1967—Eugene Payne, Charlotte Observer
1968—Paul Conrad, Los Angeles Times
1969—William Mauldin, Chicago Sun-Times
1970—Paul Conrad, Los Angeles Times
1971—Hugh Haynie, Louisville Courier-Journal
1972—William Mauldin, Chicago Sun-Times
1973—Paul Szep, Boston Globe
1974—Mike Peters, Dayton Daily News
1975—Tony Auth, Philadelphia Enquirer
1976—Paul Szep, Boston Globe
1977—Don Wright, Miami News
1978—Jim Borgman, Cincinnati Enquirer
1979—John P. Trever, Albuquerque Journal
1980—Paul Conrad, Los Angeles Times
1981—Paul Conrad, Los Angeles Times
1982—Dick Locher, Chicago Tribune

1983—Rob Lawlor, Philadelphia Daily News
1984—Mike Lane, Baltimore Evening Sun
1985—Doug Marlette, Charlotte Observer
1986—Mike Keefe, Denver Post
1987—Paul Conrad, Los Angeles Times
1988—Jack Higgins, Chicago Sun-Times
1989—Don Wright, Palm Beach Post
1990—Jeff MacNelly, Chicago Tribune
1991—Walt Handelsman, New Orleans Times-Picayune
1992—Robert Ariail, Columbia State
1993—Herbert Block, Washington Post
1994—Jim Borgman, Cincinnati Enquirer
1995—Michael Ramirez, Memphis Commercial Appeal
1996—Paul Conrad, Los Angeles Times
1997—Michael Ramirez, Los Angeles Times
1998—Jack Higgins, Chicago Sun-Times
1999—Mike Thompson, Detroit Free Press
2000—Nick Anderson, Louisville Courier-Journal
2001—Clay Bennett, Christian Science Monitor
2002—Mike Thompson, Detroit Free Press
2003—Steve Sack, Minneapolis Star-Tribune
2004—John Sherffius, jsherffius@aol.com
2005—Mike Luckovich, Atlanta Journal-Constitution

Index of Cartoonists

INDEX OF CARTOONISTS

Complete Your
CARTOON
COLLECTION

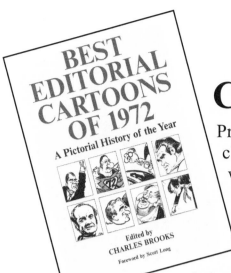

Previous editions of this timeless classic are available for those wishing to update their collection of the most provocative moments of the past three decades. Most important, in the end, the wit and wisdom of the editorial cartoonists prevail on the pages of these op-ed editorials, where one can find memories and much, much more in the work of the nation's finest cartoonists.

Select from the following supply of past editions

_____ 1972 Edition	$20.00 pb (F)	_____ 1985 Edition $20.00 pb (F)	_____ 1997 Edition $20.00 pb
_____ 1974 Edition	$20.00 pb (F)	_____ 1986 Edition $20.00 pb (F)	_____ 1998 Edition $20.00 pb
_____ 1975 Edition	$20.00 pb (F)	_____ 1987 Edition $20.00 pb	_____ 1999 Edition $20.00 pb
_____ 1976 Edition	$20.00 pb (F)	_____ 1988 Edition $20.00 pb	_____ 2000 Edition $20.00 pb
_____ 1977 Edition	$20.00 pb (F)	_____ 1989 Edition $20.00 pb (F)	_____ 2001 Edition $20.00 pb
_____ 1978 Edition	$20.00 pb (F)	_____ 1990 Edition $20.00 pb	_____ 2002 Edition $14.95 pb
_____ 1979 Edition	$20.00 pb (F)	_____ 1991 Edition $20.00 pb	_____ 2003 Edition $14.95 pb
_____ 1980 Edition	$20.00 pb (F)	_____ 1992 Edition $20.00 pb	_____ 2004 Edition $14.95 pb
_____ 1981 Edition	$20.00 pb (F)	_____ 1993 Edition $20.00 pb	_____ 2005 Edition $14.95 pb
_____ 1982 Edition	$20.00 pb (F)	_____ 1994 Edition $20.00 pb	_____ 2006 Edition $14.95 pb
_____ 1983 Edition	$20.00 pb (F)	_____ 1995 Edition $20.00 pb	_____ 2007 Edition $14.95 pb
_____ 1984 Edition	$20.00 pb (F)	_____ 1996 Edition $20.00 pb	_____ Add me to the list of standing orders

Please include $2.95 for 4th Class Postage and handling or $6.85 for UPS Ground Shipment plus $.75 for each additional copy ordered.

Total enclosed: _____

NAME _____

ADDRESS _____

CITY_____STATE_____ZIP_____

Make checks payable to:

PELICAN PUBLISHING COMPANY
1000 Burmaster St, Dept. 6BEC
Gretna, Louisiana 70053-2246

CREDIT CARD ORDERS CALL 1-800-843-1724 or or go to e-pelican.com/store
Jefferson Parish residents add 8¾% tax. All other Louisiana residents add 4% tax.
Please visit our Web site at www.pelicanpub.com or e-mail us at sales@pelicanpub.com